★ ★ ★ ★ ★

"In Dorothy's book, We Walk by Faith...Not by Sight, you will read their story of unwavering trust in the promises of the Lord and about the supernatural provision from God that has always met their needs. You will learn how to look beyond your circumstances and put your trust in Christ greater than before." — Perry Stone

WE WALK BY FAITH...
NOT BY SIGHT

Dorothy Luscombe Spaulding

DEFENDER

CRANE, MO

We Walk by Faith...Not by Sight
by Dorothy Spaulding

Defender Publishing
Crane, MO 65633
First Edition ©1997 by Dorothy Spaulding
This Edition ©2019 by Dorothy Spaulding
All Rights Reserved. Published 2019.
Printed in the United States of America.

ISBN: 978-1-948014-26-7

A CIP catalog record of this book is available from the Library of Congress.

Cover illustration and design by Jeffrey Mardis.

Dedication

"To God Be All the Glory for the Great Things He Has Done"

To my children, Brian and Sonia, Tamara and Chris, Steve and Debbie, who have faithfully stood by me all these years.

To my grandchildren, Tiffany, Lauryn, Alex, Noah, Adam, Angela, Michael, Timothy, Rebecca, Abby and Drew, who, should the Lord tarry, will carry the Good News Gospel to their generation.

To wonderful parents who have loved me and taught me the ways of the Lord. It was their faithful prayers that carried me through all my years. For that, and so much more, I thank them.

To my dear husband, Russell, who heard the call to walk the cross with a lady pulling a little red wagon and obeyed the call.

A Word from Perry Stone

Often life has been referred to as a journey. As Christians we travel life's journey by faith striving toward an eternal reward. During my ministry I have often met people on this journey of faith who truly amaze me. This is how I feel about Russell and Dorothy Spaulding.

In Dorothy's book, *We Walk by Faith...Not by Sight*, you will read their story of unwavering trust in the promises of the Lord and about the supernatural provision from God that has always met their needs. You will learn how to look beyond your circumstances and put your trust in Christ greater than before.

I have known Russell and Dorothy for over 30 years, and I believe you will be amazed, just as I have been, at their walk of faith. From their testimony of walking the cross throughout America, to building Christian television stations, and to just simply believing the Lord for the impossible, I believe you, too, will be astonished! The Bible instructs us all to walk by faith, not by sight, so today I encourage you to allow this book to inspire your life journey, and to trust the Lord greater than ever before as you too walk by faith...

Dr. Perry Stone
Voice of Evangelism Outreach Ministries
Cleveland, Tennessee

A Word from Arthur and Denise Blessitt

We Walk by Faith...Not by Sight. A provocative book of fun, truth, tears, struggle and triumph.

This book will "connect" with every reader. From Dorothy's heart and experiences come the story of a real adventure in faith.

Simon of Cyrene helped carry the cross of Jesus to Calvary. Today, Dorothy and Russell are one of the few in history to have ever taken the call of Jesus literally: "take up your cross and follow me" (Matthew 16:24; Mark 8:34; Luke 9:23).

Individually, Dorothy and Russell are beautiful people and pure followers of Jesus, but together as "one" they are a wonderful team for the glory of God. We are honored to be their true friends. They are sincere in motive, powerful in witness, firm in commitment, full of the Holy Spirit and overflowing in love for God and people.

Dorothy is full of joy which makes her so attractive to hurting people.

Follow this amazing story of triumph and strength. You'll be blessed and perhaps changed as you encounter the living Christ in the lives of these who truly seek to follow Him,

Fellow pilgrims and cross-carrying followers of Jesus.

Arthur and Denise Blessitt

The couple who walked the cross around the world

Acknowledgements

To Pastor Tim Gilligan who, by his example and anointed teaching of the Word of God, has taught us how to walk in supernatural victory, integrity and excellence in ministry. We love you and honor you.

To Arthur and Denise Blessitt, for challenging and encouraging us to keep on going.

Thank you, Daddy, for choosing to be a pastor instead of playing professional baseball and, Mother, for all your love and hard work and always being there for us girls. I love you both so much.

The Conversation

Tucked secure at the foot of the bed
I overheard
What two tennis shoes said.

"She walked us hard today.
You'd think she'd find an easier way.
My sole's in pain, I think I'll
Never walk again."
Said Lefty.

"But did you see the man she fed,
And did you hear the things she said?
She spoke about her Lord, who died.
She said a prayer—and the man cried."
Said Righty.

"But couldn't she ride and get there fast?
That way, we could last 'n last.
At this rate, we can't stay brand new.
I like my looks—don't know about you."
Said Lefty.

"Hold your tongue and listen to me!
When she speaks of the man from Galilee,
She speaks of One born in poverty,

Who gave His life to set souls free.
She follows in His steps, you see.
That's what she does, our Dorothy.
She lives to fulfill others' needs,
When she shares the Scriptures and intercedes.
And you can see that special glow,
Walking with Dorothy, day by day."
Said Righty.

Said Lefty, "I'm glad."
"Me too," said Righty.

—*Lois Wilson, October 5, 1989*

Contents

A Change in Plans
Gettysburg to Portland, Maine
Pastor Ready to Quit
Coatsville, Pennsylvania
The Billy Graham Crusade
Philadelphia
A Word to Pastors and to Sheep
Broken Lives Fit for the King
New York City Here We Come!
What Kind of Bicycle Are You Carrying!
Help, Lord!
The Ministry
Capture the Moment
A Mess All the Way Around
God's Loving On Us
Spiritual Warfare
Providence, Rhode Island
Strength from Heaven
Norwich
Circuit Riding Preacher
Boston
God's Provisions

Introduction

Where does one begin to express the mighty things that our Heavenly Father does for us his children? It is with a grateful heart to Him that I write about the way He has led my life.

This book is from my diary. Because I have retained the character of a diary, some of the reading will seem to jump.

The first chapters in this book describe what led up to the many things that happened in my life to cause me to be able to forsake things, leave it all, and walk with a wooden cross around our nation. Some of the stories will make you laugh, others will make you cry, but as you read, open your heart to hear what God may be telling you to do.

This book will show you God's constant provision and protection and will lead you into a deeper walk with Him. It will help you learn to know Him and His ways and trust Him for everything.

"For we walk by faith, not by sight"
2 CORINTHIANS 5:7

What Happened

As a child, at 10 years old, I was saved in a little mountain church. My father was both a pastor and evangelist and I heard the salvation message many times, but this time the Holy Ghost dealt with me and I wept, repenting before my Lord.

I loved God and served Him as I was growing up. I was a youth pastor, nurse on the mission field and did whatever I could in the ministry.

As the years went on, I was drawn away from the things of God by my own desires to be a success. I became a workaholic working 12–14 hours a day, every day, building a shopping center, flying here and there, demonstrating for Disney World or at a National Trade Show somewhere. I owned a retail business that I had for fourteen years. It was very successful. I had a weekly TV show on ABC, Gainesville, Florida, that ran successfully for nine years. Also, I had a weekly newspaper column for some of the New York Times papers that ran successfully for ten years. There was one accomplishment after another.

Soon Sundays became like any other work day. Day-by-day I grew further away from the things of God. As for Bible and prayer time, well, that became a rare commodity. Oh, yes, if you would ask me of my relationship with Jesus, I could tell you I was saved and that I loved God. I had fooled all those around me including myself. I was so blinded by hiding my sins in a closet, that others around me thought I was a good Christian lady.

Then at the height of this success story, I allowed sin to come into my life. I went through a divorce and found myself in what seemed to be on a land slide to the bottom. The Bible says *"the wages of sin is death"* (Romans 6:23). I planted a lot of bad seeds and there would be a harvest to reap! You will reap what you sow. We want the quick fix! Read the whole chapter of Mark 4, it's all about confession. You're the sower, you sow or plant the word with the confession of your mouth, and I planted a lot of bad seeds.

Other than my three beautiful children, my parents and friends who stood by me during those hard times, life had no meaning. Praise God—He brought me across the path of PTL—who took me in—loved on me and helped me to see that through Christ Jesus I can make it! I truly repented and gave my life totally to the Lord. Then I met a pastor named Leslie Hale who taught me how to walk in the Word of God in a way I never knew before.

When I finally came back to take over my business, it was no longer the lucrative business I once had, but instead it had a great indebtedness. Attorneys, one after the other, said the only hope I had was to go bankrupt. Because of a godly upbringing, praying parents, and because I know the God I serve says in Philippians 4:19, *"My God shall supply all my needs"* I said "No, God will help me through this." It wasn't easy, but I stood.

When I discovered the state I was in financially, I began praying for a creative idea to free me from this financial burden, thanking God for it, and claiming God's promises, this verse especially, *"What things so ever ye desire, when you pray, believe that ye receive them, and ye shall have them"* (Mark 11:24). I prayed, I believed, and God delivered.

Preparing for the Battles Ahead

Being Spirit filled, I now had a new determination to serve my Heavenly Father as never before. I would hold prayer and praise meetings in both my home and store. The Word of God says that Joshua won the battle with praise (Joshua 6). Jehoshaphat, when all evidence looked impossible around him, did as God instructed—he sent out the praisers and the victory was his (2 Chronicles 20:3–25). I needed victory over this great indebtedness, so I fought the daily battle by confessing the Word of God, prayer and praises.

When there is a battle to be won, a good soldier must be prepared. It's important during these times to focus our eyes on Jesus—and on what the Word has to say about our problem, and not on the problem for example, for finances, Philippians 4:19, for healing, Isaiah 53:4–5. Since I had wasted so many years, I had much to learn. So for those past years most of my time was spent studying God's Word, praying and learning everything I could about God's love for me, His promises and His Word. It was nothing for me to travel miles by car just to learn more about my wonderful Father. During those first eight months, I never watched any secular television, only filling myself with God's Word and praises. My friends all thought I had really flipped out! However, I believe it's so important that we guard what goes into our eyes and ears. It was also during this time that God showed me that He was going to meet my every need.

Day By Day Walk

These months weren't always easy for me. Many a night I would lie in my bed, crying out, "Help me God!" The loneliness and all the pressures sometimes were so hard to bear. In desperation and because I was hurting so badly, I would call the *700 Club* or *PTL* in the middle of the night and a prayer warrior would pray with me, always making things better.

Sometimes I would just get out of bed and, even though I didn't feel like it, I would begin praising God and dancing before him. Soon new strength would come. The Word of the Lord says in Nehemiah 8:10, *"The joy of the Lord is your strength."* As the days went on, things continually got better. You know, sometimes we expect God just to come in and wipe away all the bad and make everything good, but it doesn't always happen that way. It's a day-by-day walk with Him, knowing in due season, He will work it out for our good. Always remember *"after Abraham patiently endured, he received the promise"* (Hebrews 6:15). God will deliver you!

My Family

Tammy—Because of the divorce and the drastic lifestyle changes that occurred, my 15-year-old daughter had the hardest time. She began hanging around with the wrong kids at school. Soon she got into heavy rock music, drinking and smoking behind my back and going to the punk rock bars and gay bars in a city an hour away. She would come home all hours of the night. I, along with friends, took authority over the devil and commanded him to loose her. We would pray for her, but mostly through all of this mess, I would love her, realizing that the rebellious spirit in her was coming from hurts of the past and the rock music. I would do kind things for her, not "buying her" or approving her actions, but showing her that I loved her unconditionally.

Then one night I made her go to church with me in another city and praise God, she gave her life back to the Lord. She said, "Mother, for me to get straight, I can't stay in my school; please send me to a Christian school." I didn't have the money but I didn't care what it cost, she was going. So we began praying. That week we were told about Victory Christian School in Tulsa, Oklahoma. I called and wonderful things happened. I can't begin to tell you all the ways God provided, but in a nutshell, my friends put up the money and she got a roommate to help share expenses. Every consecutive year after that God supernaturally furnished the money for her to go to school.

In her junior year we even had less money than the year before. I told Tammy to pack her bags. She was going. God would just have to provide the money and the place to stay. That Sunday afternoon a lady came to the house and gave me a check for $1,000 for Tammy's tuition, another friend gave me $250, and others gave smaller amounts and again her way was paid. On Wednesday I had a farewell party for her. That same day, the Dean of Students called and said they wanted her to stay with them. That year she was a straight A student. I got letters from each of her teachers, along with her principal, saying what a blessing she was to the school and also how she had been a Spiritual Leader. PRAISE THE LORD!

That summer Tammy called before coming home from school, telling me that she would like to spend her summer serving God, and did I have any ideas? I suggested Continental Singers. She had been praying that if God wanted her to do this, I would say Continental Singers. The touring for the group was only two weeks away—there was money to be raised as well as their having an opening for her. So I called them. They said they only had a light technician job open but she would have to be approved first. I gave him the phone number of the school. The recommendation was so good, they immediately accepted her. Well, Tammy's summer was one fantastic story after another of how God provided for her.

Brian—My oldest son, an excellent saxophonist, desired to travel for two summers with the Continental Singers. The first summer we had just a few weeks to raise $4,000 for his trip. God, supernaturally, intervened with many friends.

The second year when he wanted to go, all positions for sax players were taken. I will never forget how his face dropped in disappointment when he heard the news. I said, "Brian, God can change this for you. He wants to show himself faithful." So we prayed and applied Mark 11:24

and believed God. A few days later The Continental Singers leader called and said one of the girls who played both tenor and alto sax had heard of Brian. He said she would play the alto sax, therefore leaving the door open for Brian to play tenor sax on the Norway Tour. That day a man walked into my store and gave me $5,000 for Brian, which not only paid his way but helped pay the way for another girl who didn't have all her money.

Steve—My youngest son, Steve, at 15, rededicated his life to the Lord and became Spirit filled. He is a very good drummer and from that time forward he began playing faithfully for our church every Sunday. One summer he played for a traveling Tent Ministry. Steve had chances to play for secular rock bands but he decided to play for the Lord. God has also provided for him many times when we didn't have money.

I can remember one time right after Steve had given his life back to the Lord, he had gone to a fair and won a Madonna poster which he brought home and placed on his bedroom wall. I walked into his room and, seeing the poster, told Steve to get it off his wall and throw it away. He said okay, but never did.

Within days Steve become very ill. The doctor said it was Mono and he was getting weaker by the day. We anointed him with oil and prayed, but still, he was getting weaker. A few days later I walked into the room and the poster laughed at me! I told this to Steve and he promised he would get rid of it. That night when I walked into his room I noticed the poster had been taken down.

I know that we can allow curses to come upon us when we place ungodly things in our homes. I thought perhaps that hanging the Madonna poster was the reason he got so sick. However, as the days passed no one could give me any answers as to why Steve was so ill. I could feel the spirit of death on him.

One night, while he was sleeping, I went into his room and began binding up the spirit of death over him, when all of a sudden Steve sat straight up in his bed, still asleep, and said, "It's behind the dresser," and lay back down. I looked behind the dresser and there was the poster of Madonna. I took the poster outside, burned it and said, "In the name of Jesus, I break any curse you have placed on my son and I command you in Jesus' name to loose him and set him free." Screams came out of that poster as it burned. Immediately, my son was totally healed.

When we as Christians bring in cursed, ungodly things into our homes, we open the door for Satan to work in our lives. I know because I experienced it firsthand.

The Business and Ministry

Those past years in the natural, had been some of the hardest in my life. But God's constant provision and love for us can make us overcomers. The answers to prayers are so many I can hardly begin to tell you all of them, but I will share with you a few.

Ministry in the Store

I could feel God really changing things in my life. The business that I once loved and held so dear no longer had the meaning it used to have, but rather, I would find myself looking for ways that I could help meet the needs of others.

As sick people came into the store I would tell them what the Word said. I would pray for them and many would be healed instantly. Soon people started bringing friends into the sore to be ministered to in one fashion or another.

I remember one afternoon, a lady came into the store with tears in her eyes and I asked if I could please pray for her. She then proceeded to tell me how her husband called her from Washington, D.C. in regards to a court case. Their attorney told them he felt there was no hope and they would lose everything. Well, the Spirit of God rose up in me and I said, "I don't receive that bad report." These people were Christians and I knew the power of prayer and agreement. So we prayed and agreed, spoke the Word over the situation, and one week later they both came into the store praising God. They had supernaturally won the case.

There are so many things like this that happened in the store.

One day Rafie, a doctor's son that I had been ministering to, said, "You have got to go down to the hospital and pray for this boy who was riding a bike and got hit by a semi-truck." He said the doctors didn't think he would make it through the night. So I said, "Let's just pray now." We agreed together that God would spare his life and heal him.

Later that night I was on my way to church when the Spirit of God spoke to me and told me to go lay hands on the boy and pray for him. I said, "Father, I will go but you must open the door for me to get into ICU where he is." When arriving at the intensive care waiting room, I saw a man with his head bowed into his hands. He had been weeping. I said to the man, "Do you know if there is a young boy in ICU who was hit by a truck?" He said, "Yes, he is my nephew."

I proceeded to tell him God sent me there with a message for him. He was going to live and not die. I showed him Mark 16:17 and 18 where it says, "And these signs shall follow them that believe; In my name...they shall lay hands on the sick and they shall recover." The man was so thrilled by the news that he took me into a room where the boy's mother, father and family were.

They were all crying. I knew the first thing I had to do was to pray peace on them. They listened intently as I told them what the Word of God said about their son. Then they took me into the ICU and there lay little Bazoid, their son, lifeless and in a coma.

I immediately bound the spirit of death on him as I laid hands on him and prayed for his total healing. I then said, "Bazoid, you will live and not die because Jesus had healed you." I told his family to see Bazoid as healed and, no matter what reports the doctor would give, they were to say, "Jesus healed Bazoid."

Now I must tell you these people were from India and were Hindu, but they believed the good report that Jesus healed Bazoid!

The next night, I went in again to see Bazoid, and he still lay there lifeless but I just laid hands on him and praised God for his healing. On my way out of the room a nurse said to me, "He's not going to make it." I said, "He will live and walk again."

Days later, the doctors called the family to come to the hospital because Bazoid wasn't going to make it until morning. Bazoid's family said, "No, Jesus healed Bazoid." Such faith they had in those few words I was able to share with them! The doctor said if he lived he would be a vegetable. Again, they refused to believe that report. One day, a few months later, little Bazoid came walking into my store with his family and he grabbed my legs and hugged me. I asked him who healed him and he said, "Jesus." Praise the Lord for such faith.

A great lesson for all of us to remember is: *"Who hath believed our report?"* (Isaiah 53:1) that is, whose report will you believe? I choose to believe the report of the Lord! The Word says, *"As he thinketh in his heart so is he"* (Proverbs 23:7). It's with the heart we believe the Word and what it says.

God Sends Encouragement

The financial pressure at this time just kept getting worse. Daily family and friends would say, "File bankruptcy!" and I would always say that God is more than able to deliver me.

One day my Heavenly Father brought a Christian truck driver into the store to minister to me. Truthfully, for months I thought he was an angel. From the moment he walked into the store until he left, out of his mouth came the Word and it hit me squarely between the eyes. He came at a weak moment in my life when I was about ready to throw in the towel. He told me that God sent him to speak to me. He had never been there before and when he prayed for me, we knelt right there in the middle of the floor. I came out of there stronger than ever.

Working with Kids

Soon a new ministry started in the store and that was working with high school and gay kids. All of a sudden, it seemed like there were so many of them. They came from the very elite families to the hard core street kids. They all needed the same thing—LOVE.

Many parents today are just not spending quality time in loving their children.

Soon I became known as "Mom" to all the kids. They were getting saved left and right. It was great! We would spend Friday and Saturday evenings going out and working with the kids on the streets and so many of them would receive the Gospel. They were hungry for the Word. God gave me such a heart for these teenagers. Weekly, I would bring them to church, filling up one and two rows. Being a single mom, I got a lot of flak from some of the members of the church. They would tell me it wasn't right for me to have all those teenagers come into my home, especially the young boys. So I begged some of the men of the church to work with these teens and I backed off. However, no one would take the time for them and soon some quit coming to church.

Always do what you think God is telling you to do. Don't be led by what others say.

Town Square

I had gotten a report that some of the young boys I had worked with were down on the town square, prostituting. I was so angry at the devil that I went down to the square with several other kids to see if the report was really true. I was amazed when I saw many young men gathered together on a bench near a pay phone. I got out of my van and walked up into the middle of them. Several of the boys who recognized me felt somewhat ashamed that I saw them there. The leader of the group spoke up, "Who are you and what do you want here?" I said, "These are my kids and I've come to get them." He proceeded to tell me that he was the mother and they would obey whatever he said.

Just then the phone rang and he said, "Greg, go get that phone," so off he went. I said, "Greg, are you going to let this guy tell you what to do?" Stopping for a moment, he looked at me. Then the leader yelled out and off he went.

I told the leader that, starting that night and every night thereafter, I would be down at the square until they either gave their hearts to Jesus or moved out of our city. They were not going to be allowed to work there any longer and destroy any more young boys' lives.

So I began to preach and pray. At first they jeered, but soon they all took off in different directions. Night after night, we would go down to the square and sometimes we would just walk around the square and pray. Towards the end, they would literally run when there saw me coming. It wasn't too long until they were completely gone. We were able to rescue some, but others were lost to homosexuality. Greg, by the way, died of AIDS at the age of 26 years old.

Christians, stand up and be counted. You don't have to allow the devil to reign on your block.

You can call the peace of God to abide where you live. You can make a difference!

The Store

Things were really bad, so I asked intercessors to come in the mornings and pray over the store. At one time I even hired an intercessor and, daily, God would deliver me out of one crisis after another.

The Sales Tax Incident

There was one particular time I remember, when the sales tax people came into the store. As they did so many times before, they would make me feel so bad. However, this time they were going to take an inventory and close me up. I went to the man and said, "Please don't do this, Paul. I know God will deliver me, I just need more time." He couldn't take it and left.

A few days later he came back with his boss, and this time, his boss was so hard on me in front of my customers that I started to cry. I didn't know what to do so I just went to the back of the store and cried out to God. He impressed me to call Tallahassee.

When I called Tallahassee I told them what happened. God gave me favor and they were no longer able to harass me. PRAISE GOD!

That Christmas I was able to pay them off and, praise God, Paul the tax man said, "Dorothy, I don't know anyone else who would have stood so strong for so long and paid it off." I said, "It's Jesus in me."

The Rent

One time I had to have $8,000 rent within four days or they were going to close me up. I called all my friends and we all wrote our particular needs on a piece of paper. We laid hands on them and prayed over them, we bound up the devil and went to battle with praise to God. That was a Tuesday night. Wednesday night when we closed the store, I said, "Everyone go home, I will see you later." I walked through the store praising God for what He was doing.

Several hours had gone by and a friend, whom I had not heard from in months, called me and asked me why I was there so late. I told her I was praising God for the victory that was going to take place by noon the next day. She really had no reason to call except to talk.

The next morning my family, along with well-meaning friends, came to the store and said they wanted to rent a truck and empty the store of $200,000 worth of merchandise, so when they locked the store, we'd still have some of the merchandise. I said, "NO! God will provide!" not knowing where it would come from. At noon the lady I talked with the night before and another friend came into the store and each had a check and together they amounted to the $8,000 I needed. Praise God!

Things Aren't Always Great

Oftentimes we can be like the children of Israel. When we see God's provisions daily, we rejoice, however, when we come to the Red Sea, we weaken and take things in our own hands.

Perhaps the Red Sea experience can come because we haven't completely learned to walk in His complete rest (trusting Him fully).

A few months before the $8,000 issue, I had my 1-year-old van repossessed. Basically what happened was, I took off for a meeting and my bookkeeper made the deposits into my personal account as usual.

Well, a new bank president took over and took the money from my personal account and placed it into the store account. This bounced 35 of my checks which, in cash, amounted to a little over $600 in bounced check charges. So I told my bookkeeper not to make the van payment until I got back.

When I came home I went down to talk to the president of that particular bank. This was on a Thursday. On Monday morning the sales tax people, as they had done several times before, took the money from my store account. This frightened the new bank president so she had my van repossessed, which was only about a half a month late.

Shocked and not understanding, I forgot about praising God and I cried out, "Why God?"

The next morning a friend came into the store and brought a certified check for three months van payments which covered the past due month, the month we were in and a month in advance.

My bookkeeper and I took it down to the president of the bank, but she would not accept it. They took and sold the van for half what it was worth. Even in this, I had to learn to praise God.

Sales would go from bad to worse. Nothing seemed to work anymore. It was only our prayers and God's continual blessing that kept us going.

In May a huge new Ben Franklin store opened right across the street. Whatever I would put up in my window for sale he would top it. Things looked bad. It used to be I would take on any competition because I had the money to play the game but it seemed as though I was stripped from everything. God placed in me an inner strength that helped me make it through those hard days.

New Owners, New Problems

In May of that year, new owners bought the shopping center. For those of us who had been there 10 years or more we didn't have leases so they immediately doubled our rents, effective July 1.

I could not pay this new rent and, again, I was faced with being locked up. I just stood on God's Word and believed Him. At this point He was my only hope.

On the day this amount was due, I drove down to Tampa to meet with the people in charge of the center. They said if the rent was not in their hands by 4:00 they would have to lock up my store. So I called back to the store and said, "I've done all I can do; now it's up to God."

Meanwhile, the lady who owned the store next to mine, called my friends and told them the story. By the time I got back to Ocala, people had poured into her shop giving her $100 each. Some of the people gave when they didn't have it to give. Again, as He had so many times before, the Lord gave us the victory. Praise His name for ever more!

New Location

In September, we received a letter stating that we had to sign a lease with double the rent plus $35,000 for improvements or we had to be out of the center by September 30.

Knowing the greater volume of my business is made October through December, a move right then would be unheard of. So I began to paint the store, put up new drapes and believed that God would work it out, as He had done so many times in the past.

On September 13, my mother leaned over the register and began to cry. She said, "I can't take it anymore, you act like nothing is happening and you must do something." So that morning on the way to the bank I cried out to God and said, "God, if I've missed it, I'm sorry. Please God, for my mother's sake, open another door."

All of a sudden, I made a turn up a road I very rarely travelled into the Ocala Historic district. There stood a beautiful 98-year-old house.

I knew then that the Lord had led me as He had so many times before. He then gave me the idea of trading our Christmas decorations for the owner's home or office in exchange for the rent from September 15 to January 15, at which time we would renegotiate for the new rent or purchase of the building.

Joy began to come over me for I knew this was of God. That afternoon, I presented the idea to the owner's sister and she said that he'd never go for it and I said, "If it's God, it will work." She then said that they had not heard from her brother for some weeks but when she could get a hold of him she would present him with the idea.

She no more than spoke those words when her brother called, as I was sitting there, and he said, "Go for it." That was Wednesday afternoon. On Friday I signed the paper and on Saturday we got a letter from the owner of the shopping center saying we had to be out in three days.

I called the street kids, my parents, friends and customers to help and within three days we were completely moved out of a 3,200 square foot store. We had people working around the clock and no one would take a dime for it. God had truly blessed me with friends.

The first night before moving we walked into the new store and anointed it to the glory of God and dedicated the business to the Lord.

Setting Up the New Store

I had no idea how to fix up that old house to look like a store, as it was so different from anything I'd ever worked with. It had three stories, 18 rooms, nine fire places, three upstairs porches, two kitchens, two baths, and a large grand hall with an open winding staircase.

I walked through the rooms while they were still empty and God showed me just what to do. I was able to see it completed before the first thing was in the room. We took all the old shelving, lattice work and dividers from the old store, cut it apart and reworked it so that I did not have to buy the first piece of wood and, to top that off, one of the boys that called me "Mom" was a carpenter and he took off several days from his work to build the shelves for me. My father also helped with much of the carpentry and again no one took a dime.

Customers and friends worked day and night to help me get the store ready for our grand opening. I'd get to work at 7:00 in the morning and five to fifteen people would come and volunteer their time.

The new store was so beautiful and blessed of the Lord. We prospered there. The first of December when we decorated the owner's house we spared nothing, investing $3,800.00 worth. We told him how good we were doing at the new store, and wanted to work something out where we could keep it. We were assured that something could be worked out.

It was a real show place and people would come from cities all over to see it. Our sales increased and it seemed as though the worst was over and we were going to make it. I was able for the first time to start paying off some bills. We had a great Christmas season. We decorated for the attraction at Silver Springs as well as many other homes and businesses.

Shocking Days

Then one day in December, a huge "For sale" sign went up in front of my beautiful new store. I couldn't understand it. I called the owner but he would never return my calls. Then I spoke to his sister and said, "You know I want to keep this place." She said, "But you can't afford it." I said, "I know God will work something out!" Meanwhile, I prayed, "God, You know my needs and I thank You for this beautiful store and the great business. I now commit this store and my future totally into Your hands and I will rest in You."

January 14 the shock really came. At 5:00 p.m. the owner's sister came into the store and said they had another purpose for the house and we would have to be out in one week. I couldn't believe my ears.

The customers standing there, who heard it all, were as shocked as I was. Perhaps that was why my many phone calls to the owner were never returned.

Calling On God For Direction

That night my children, Tammy and Steve, who were to leave to go to school in Tulsa the next week, and I sat on the floor, held hands and prayed, "God, help us, lead and show us exactly what to do."

At this point, with no business and no job, and me being the provider for my family, plus the heavy financial burden of the past, everything seemed to be falling in around me and for the first time in my life I really felt helpless. I felt numb to everything, it was like I was just existing. I didn't feel like praising God, but we all gave the sacrifice of praise.

Selling Out

The next day, I reduced everything to half price and said we were selling out. People were shocked, after all I had been in business for 14 years. The general public never knew of the great financial pressure I was under and they just could not understand.

Our new store seemed to be so successful and a real show place in Ocala. The Chamber of Commerce had just taken pictures of the store for their new brochure. The store was probably one of the most photographed places in Ocala. Even the owner told us how well pleased he was with it.

I had business people in town who, when they heard what happened, offer me places to sell my things and open a new store saying, "Don't quit now." Others would drive me around town looking for places, but I did what I felt in my heart God wanted me to do. It was a real step of faith.

God Provided

We managed to get a two week extension, and in the middle of all of this, God provided the money for the children to go to school in Tulsa. So I took them, resting in the fact that I was in God's perfect will.

On moving day, when I had to move the store to my house and six storage units, once again God provided along with all the friends who helped me so many times in the past.

God sent two men from Ohio and Virginia to Ocala to help me. They called my mother and asked if she had a typewriter because they need to type some legal documents. They explained that they were friends of some friends of my parents, so she let them come over. While they were there, she told them about me. They stayed in town two extra days just to help me move. They worked very energetically from early morning on into the night, and, again, at no charge.

Isn't God wonderful?

The Prophecy

As the days began in February, I would cry out to God and ask Him what it was He wanted me to do. Then early one morning, February 16, here's what He said to me.

Dorothy, you have done well, these are new beginnings for you. Continue to seek My face and learn of Me. I will lead you in the way you are to go. The love of God will reign strong in you and you will be able to accomplish those things which I have called you to do.

You will walk in My perfect way. Beware of those things which so easily beset you. Know that I, the Lord your God, am in you and with you. I will guide you in all truths. Fret not about the things that have gone by. Now is a time of new beginnings.

Be strong and learn of Me and you will truly be the woman I have chosen you to be. Don't let the cares of this life or the natural things of this life hold you back but walk in My Spirit, go forth and preach the Gospel to the needy, to those who are down-trodden, to those who have been pushed aside as rejects.

For here, there are no rewards of men, but My rewards are far greater. I will cover you and protect you as you stand and go forth into the ghetto areas, feeding My sheep the Word, giving them food and clothing.

Be a shepherd to the hurting. Dorothy, do these things and I will lift you up to do greater things. Walk not after the things of the flesh, but after the Spirit.

Make your house a house of prayer. I look for willing vessels to use. So now go forth and do even that which I've committed into your hands. I love you, My child.

Definite Direction

With that, my heart leaped with joy because for the first time since all of the moving, I finally had a direction to go. That very week I drove to Crystal River every night, about an hour away, to hear Dave Roberson.

Remember this prophecy came on Monday morning. Wednesday evening in that meeting there was a man named John Solomon from Daytona Beach, who got up and talked about Street Reach. Tears came to my eyes and I began to weep. What he had just talked about matched up with my prophecy exactly. Later that week Dave Roberson laid hands on me and said I was a chosen one. I knew what I had to do.

Street Reach

So the following Thursday evening, I showed up on Daytona Beach, which was two hours away, and I began working with Street Reach. From that time on, I was in charge of the feeding program. People that came were tramps, alcoholics, street people, punk rockers, and Satan worshippers. We loved them all just like they were, and also, we showed them the love of Jesus. After all, that was what they were really searching for.

As the Lord led me I would open with a few words of ministry. Then we would pray and tell them that If anyone wanted to know more about this Jesus we spoke about to talk to us after the meal. It was great because a group of them would gather around and ask questions.

We were their servants while they ate. We fed them as much as they wanted. After eating, they could take showers and get clean clothes.

Many of them had never been treated so well and so they all wanted to do something for us. Several would come around every day and work around the church. One of them bought a bottle of shampoo for the shower. It was really a blessing to see. When people give their lives to Jesus the first thing they want to do is give.

Changes in Me

I love what God has done in my life and for using me in this way. People are getting saved so easily now. Praise God!

I could tell you story after story about the street people, how they got there, why they are the way they are, etc. Praise God, He's made a Street Preacher out of me. He's given me such a love for the kids and the street people, and to win them to Jesus is the greatest joy one could ever experience.

When you are hurting, give out of yourself to others less fortunate and you will forget about your problems.

I marvel at the changes God has made in me. I can't explain it. It's like the Spirit of God has just taken over, and I'm along for the ride. Please understand it's not the same ME. I've changed. All that matters is Jesus and the fact that there is a world that is lost and going to hell and needs to hear and see the love of Jesus.

One day I was probably paid the highest compliment, and that was from a fellow worker who hasn't always been the sweetest person. He said, "When I see you, I see the love of Jesus." Praise God, because that is my deepest desire.

The pressures of the past seem to get lighter and I know the day will come when they will be totally wiped away to the glory of God.

The Bride

As I said earlier, I had been praying for a creative idea.

In the summer when everything around me looked so dark, as I described earlier, just before I moved my store to the Historical District, my friend, Ruby, constantly insisted that I paint a resurrection picture.

I told her that I didn't paint people, but she wouldn't quit. One day, she brought me a large canvas and said, "Paint." So to keep her quiet, I finally said I would.

That Sunday afternoon I placed the canvas board on the easel. Then I lay down on the floor, face down, and cried out to God. I had no idea what to paint or what colors to use. He had to help me.

After some time in prayer, I got up and put the tape of Mike Atkins' "Messiah" on. It played over and over again. I put the colors on the palette and began to paint, just praising God the whole time along with the tape and never really concentrating on what I was painting.

About an hour or so later, there was this beautiful background that God had given me to paint. I was so taken in by it and immediately signed it HGI—Holy Ghost Inspired—to give credit where it is due.

That evening while sitting in church again, things began to come to me—I could see Jesus, the bride, and some angels, but wasn't sure how to place it on the canvas.

The canvas, with the background on it, sat in the back of the store for a week. Whenever people would see it they would know it was heaven without me saying a word. "Praise God!" I would say, "He's answered my prayer. He's given me a creative idea to bless others, as well as myself."

The next Saturday I decided to finish the painting. However; I didn't want to mess up the original and since I am a copy artist, I thought I would copy it and do another one. I worked all day Saturday and into the evening, and could not get the same feel of the painting I had done earlier. So I cleaned up my brush and laid it aside.

The next day, while I was praising God for all He had done for me, I heard a Voice saying, "I didn't give you a copy but the original. Take up your brush and I will guide it."

With that I took up my brush, again playing the tape, and praising God. Two evenings later I had a finished painting. He truly led me all the way, showing me one part at a time until it was finished.

While the painting was still wet we anointed it with oil and had the whole church agree that it would touch the hearts of the people and would lead many to salvation from all nations.

You Have to Give to Receive

Now that I had this beautiful painting there would have to be copies made in order to get it out into people's homes. After checking into the printing cost it seemed impossible as I didn't have the money. I again prayed and cast the care of it into Jesus' hands.

Within days I heard of Christian people who were color printers in Clearwater, Florida. When I was quoted the price for printing, I needed a real miracle. The day the painting was to be taken down to Clearwater, there wasn't any money for printing.

I cried, "Lord, what do you want me to do?" He laid it on my heart to take all my gold jewelry, put it in a box and take it to the printers. So with confidence in the Lord and with my wet painting, off I went. The printer sat there and put her head down and said, "This must be God. I've never done something like this before, but I know it's what I must do." Joy sprang up in me and I just began to praise God. I had to be willing to give up a great treasure and God honored it! Praise the Lord!

God Promotes the Painting

Now that I had the prints, there had to be a way of putting them out in the market area. The best magazine I could find was Charisma. After speaking with the people from Charisma they told me they were all sold out for the Christmas issue. I said, "If God wants me to have a page for this print, He will open one up."

Two days later I received a phone call from Charisma. They said, strangely, they had some extra page to open up. Knowing it was by the hand of God, they said I could have it for $2,300. Regular cost was around $6,000. I shouted for joy. I said, "I'll take it! When do you need the money?" This was Friday and they needed it by Tuesday morning. In faith, and knowing God was doing this, I said, "You'll have it!"

You must remember that I was completely broke. Again, I went to prayer and confessing God's Word over this situation.

Tuesday morning a lady walked into my store and laid 23 one-hundred-dollar bills on my counter and said she was in an investment meeting the night before and that God spoke to her heart to give me this amount of money because I had need of it!

"To God Be the Glory for the Great Things He Has Done!"

When the orders came in, I was able to take the money I made, go down and pay the printers and guess what, she had saved my jewelry for me and gave it back.

Praise the Lord!

Dark Days Ahead

After closing the store in January there are no words to describe how I felt. In the natural it seemed all was lost. I was a single mother of three children, two of which were in school in Tulsa with no means of support except for the few Bride print orders that were slowly coming in. God would have to move. I had to trust Him for everything.

We continued ministering on the street at night, and during the day, I would try to sell things out of my garage and storage units for ten cents on the dollar of what they cost me. I would set up my things in different friends' yards. The rains would come and thousands of dollars would be lost. I cried, "God, what do you want from me?"

A friend brought me a cake that said, "To my friend, Job." That cake truly gave me hope, because I knew Job made it through his hard times and was blessed on the other side.

I would try to get jobs, but everyone would say I was over qualified. No one would hire me.

I had a crystal bell collection, probably my most valued possession. Week after week I would take these bells to the flea market selling them for less than half their value.

It was time to take the children to college. Tammy was accepted at RHEMA Bible Training Center in Broken Arrow, Steve at Oral Roberts University and at Emmanuel College, and my oldest son was going to Community College—and I only had $112 to my name.

After experiencing the mighty move of God in my life, I just knew God would provide, so off the three of us, $112 and the painting, went to Tulsa. We would stop in at bookstores and sell the prints of "The Bride" for money for food and gas.

My son, Steve, had saved up about $600 toward his year at school. So we went to register him first but, since that was all the money we had, he was turned out from both Oral Roberts and Emmanuel. Both of us sat in the car and just cried, "Why, God?"

Disappointed, hurt and broken, Steve gave his money to Tammy. We were able to set her up in a small efficiency apartment. Selling some prints, we were able to get Tammy into RHEMA.

During the days that followed, Steve and I would drive to different cities, selling the prints to have enough money for food, books, etc. I began to give up on God's help, although He had carried me through so many hard times.

Steve who was an A student, couldn't go to college because there was no provision for him. It was during one of those dark days that a friend of mine from Ocala called and said, "Dorothy, I have a large farm with empty buildings on it, come back to Ocala and I will set you up in business." So home to Ocala Steve and I went with a new excitement of going back to work.

We worked hard to prepare to open a Christmas house on the farm. It was beautiful. We sent out many invitations and, on opening day, we hired Lolly the Trolley and had valet parking. It was great!

People came from everywhere. Within five weeks we made $17,000 and we were on our way back up the success ladder. We came in with such a bang it scared the other property owners and, within weeks, the zoning board closed us down.

Again, heartbroken, I said, "Why God? I've done everything I know to do. What do you want from me?"

The only thing I knew to do was to fast and pray. With that I went on a 42-day fast of water and juice. Daily, I spent hours in the Word seeking the face of God. It was during this time that the Lord showed me I was a partner with an unbeliever.

I had given up all ministry, and had that business been allowed to go on, I would have once again grown far from God. Remember His ways are higher than our ways.

After the 42 days of fasting, I came off of it by taking communion with a dear friend and then went out and ate a steak dinner, which I might say, in the natural, you should never do after such a long fast.

God Gave Direction

The next three days I still didn't know what God wanted me to do so I went out looking for housing for street people. After looking at so many buildings I said, "Father, which one do you want?" Finally He spoke. He said, "None of them." He said, *"WALK WITH A WOODEN CROSS FROM FLORIDA TO WASHINGTON, D.C."*

Yes, I thought my heart would burst with joy. I now had direction! I asked when He wanted me to do this. He said, "Good Friday, a little over two weeks away."

Turning my car around in the middle of 8th Avenue, I headed straight to AAA, got maps, went home and began marking routes to take walking from Florida to Washington, D.C. I was so excited.

My son, Steve, came in, and seeing the maps asked, "What are you doing?" I answered, "The Lord told me to walk with a wooden cross from Florida to Washington, D.C." "No way!" he exclaimed. I answered, "Yes He did!" His answer was, "Well, I'm glad He told you and not me."

Never having walked any distance before, and in order to mark out the walk, I decided to go over to the two mile jogging track and see how long it would take me. I could walk two miles at a pretty fast pace, in half an hour. So that meant I could walk four miles an hour.

With that piece of information I marked the map according to where the cities lay, walking anywhere between 27–38 miles a day. Have you ever tried to keep up that pace for eight hours? It's a killer! I'll tell you more about that later.

The following day consisted of one phone call after another, calling friends and asking them to walk the cross with me. After all, this cross would weigh approximately 80 pounds. People thought I was crazy and no one would walk with me. After all, God had called me, not them.

One day someone gave me Arthur Blessitt's book of his walking the cross. There had to be a way to carry supplies, such as: rain gear, water, tracts and, of course, the picture of "The Bride." I looked at one idea after another when the Lord showed me a little red wagon.

That day a friend called and said, "I see you walking with a little red wagon and a man carrying the cross. On this trip you will fall in love with the man you are going to marry." Well, the confirmation of the wagon and the man carrying the cross was great. But, the part about the man I was going to marry, I wasn't too sure of that.

It was the Thursday before Palm Sunday and, still, there was no one to carry the cross with me, so I decided to go down to Daytona Beach and get a bunch of street people to go with me. I thought we could all walk and carry "Jesus" signs. There were about 13 of them who said they wanted to go. I told them they had to meet met at 6:00 Sunday morning in Ocala, at the Town Square, and we would leave from there.

A friend of mine built the cross. Now all we had to do was put the wheel on it. My father was drilling the holes for the bolts, to put the wheel on, when the drill slipped and went deep into the palm of his hand. Immediately, I grabbed his hand, and looking at it, knew he needed stitches. I commanded, in the name of Jesus, to stop bleeding and to close up. We went into the house to wash off the blood and praise God, it was totally closed up with only a line where it was cut.

My son, Steve, saw the miracle right before his eyes. You could never convince him that God does not heal.

Palm Sunday morning came and I said good-bye to my family and friends. My mother could hardly bear the idea of us walking the cross. She begged me not to go. I said, "Everything will be okay because it's what God told me to do." Excited, I went down to the square, and waited and waited. Not one person showed up. With tears streaming down my face I cried, "God, why?"

I went to church that morning and several people said in jest, "I thought you were walking the cross to Washington today." I hurt because I knew it was what God said to do.

Then a man came to me and said, "Dorothy, it's better to have done what you thought God told you to do than to do nothing!" That blessed me. That night when I was in my prayer time God spoke to me. He said, "Dorothy, why do you always do things your way? What day is it?" "Palm Sunday," I replied.

"When did I tell you to leave?" He asked. I said, "Good Friday." "You must learn to follow instructions and do things as I tell you and not your way."

It is so important that we be led by the Spirit of God!

Can you imagine what a mess I would have had on my hands had I walked with all those street people? I repented and said, "Lord, I will do anything, I commit my ways to You and believe that You will establish my thoughts. Your Word says the footsteps of the righteous man are ordered of the Lord, so therefore, I rest in You knowing that You are able to do what I cannot do."

I slept great that night. Monday morning I woke up still at peace and praising God for what He was going to do.

Russell

That morning I was surprised by a phone call from Russell Spaulding from Daytona Beach. He said, "What's this I hear about you walking with a cross from Florida to Washington, D.C.?"

I leaped with joy as I told him what God told me. I asked if he was interested in going along. He said, "Why don't I come over and we can talk and pray about it." I said, "Great!" While I was waiting what seemed to be hours, I thought about Russell and what God had done in his life.

Russell was raised Catholic as a very young child, but as the years went on he had no spiritual upbringing. By the time he was 13 years old he was running away from home and by the age of 16 he had become a full-fledged alcoholic.

While under the influence of alcohol and running with the wrong crowd, he was in and out of juvenile detention centers for theft, DUI's and all kind of juvenile criminal activity. He was just getting into one trouble situation after another. After appearing before the judge so many times he was told that one more time and he would go to jail for years.

That last time came. All seemed hopeless when the judge mercifully told him that since most of his crimes were alcohol related, if he would go through AA and go to a detention center trade school that he would let him off. Gladly, he agreed to do it.

It was while he was at the trade school a man came and ministered to the kids who were there. He told them the Good News Gospel.

When he spoke with Russell and asked him if he wanted to accept Jesus, Russell said, "Hey man, I'm in there, I'm Catholic," trying to brush the man off. But God had other plans for Russell. So by the tugging of the Holy Spirit, the man didn't leave. He persisted. "Russell," he said, "I'm not talking about a religion, I'm talking about a personal relationship with Jesus. He loves you so much and has a wonderful plan for your life."

"No way," Russell stated, "you mean I can talk to Jesus just like you and I are talking?" "Yes, you can, you don't have to go through a priest. You can go directly to Him," the man said. Russell pondered that thought. All he knew of God, was a God of wrath he could never please; he felt he would never be good enough.

Just then the man said, "Russell, in yourself you could never be good enough. But through the blood of Jesus and your acceptance of that price of Jesus dying for you, God the Father sees you clean. He wants to change your life. Give me your hand."

So Russell did and he received Jesus as his Lord and Savior. The man said, "Now, I want to baptize you!" After explaining what that meant he proceeded to baptize Russell. When Russell came up out of that water he shouted, "I feel so clean!" He was a new man. The man told him to read the Bible and pray every day.

Read? Russell hated reading and, with no teaching, after about five days he gradually slipped back into his old habits. However, he never forgot that special night.

The Work of God promises us that He will never leave us or forsake us when we slip back into sin. I believe He will always be there to bring you back to Him, and so it was with Russell.

Four years later, Russell now having been sober for approximately

2 and a half years, came to one of those hard places in his life. He had just lost his girlfriend, his job, his truck and had two weeks to move out of where he was living. Weighted down with the weight of all of his problems and with tears streaming down his face he was riding his bike on a four lane highway. The devil was bombarding his mind with thoughts of suicide.

Russell crashed his bike into the ditch, threw his hands in the air and cried out, "This world stinks! Drunk or sober, I hate this world!"

Suddenly, he saw through his mind's eye that experience he had had years prior when he accepted Jesus as his Lord and Savior. He remembered how good and clean he felt. All broken, he cried out, "I'll do anything to change my life."

Immediately, as he had felt before, a great calm came over him along with a peace he couldn't explain. He got up from that place with joy, walking with his broken down bike, and talking with the Father. Later that day he heard on the radio about Street Reach, the place where I was working with the street program.

I will never forget the first night he came. He was kind of quiet. He wanted to get involved helping the street people. We told him we were going out on the street that night and carrying sandwiches to feed the hungry and, if he wanted, he could go with us. He agreed, but he just wanted to watch. We said that would be fine, he could carry the bags of sandwiches.

Little did he know the man with the bag was whom everyone came to. So he had to get involved immediately talking to people.

That night when we went back, Pastor John asked him how he liked it. He said he loved it! Then Pastor John asked him about his acceptance of Jesus, and Russell told him all that had happened to him.

Pastor John spoke to him about the Baptism of the Holy Spirit. Russell said he wanted all he could receive of the Father. So we all gathered around to pray for Russell. The pastor laid hands on Russell and immediately he was filled with the Holy Spirit. When Russell opened his eyes, he glowed. He ran around the church shouting and praising God.

The youth pastor, Fred, asked Russell to room with him. He began to teach Russell about the Word of God.

A few days after Russell was baptized in the Holy Spirit, Fred asked Russell to go into the conference room with him. Upon doing so he said, "Russell, I believe I'm supposed to lay hands on you and pray for you." Russell agreed. The moment Fred did, Russell's knees buckled and he fell on the floor.

The next thing Russell heard was a voice saying, "Get up from there, if someone comes into the room you'd look silly lying there." Another voice said, "Lie still." Fred then began yelling at Russell and saying, "Tell me who you are?" Russell thought, "What do you mean, who am I? What's the matter with you, Fred, you know who I am. I'm Russell your roommate."

The voices came again, one saying, "Get up from there," and the other, "Stay still and don't say anything." Russell thought to himself, *What's going on here?* Meanwhile, Fred was shouting, "Come out of him in Jesus' name." Soon Russell's hands were stretching out like claws and sweat was pouring out all over him. Fred continued saying, "Come out of him in Jesus' name." By now Russell was really beside himself wondering what was going on.

All of a sudden out of Russell's mouth came a demonic voice, "I am suicide," along with loud blood-curdling screams. Fred said, "Come out of him, suicide, in Jesus' name." Within minutes Russell laid limp on the floor in a pool of sweat. "Wow, what a trip!" he said. "I have never experienced anything like that before."

Fred told Russell he had been delivered from a spirit of suicide. This totally blew Russell away. To him, the spiritual realm had become so real. He was a young man who had never been taught about the things of the spirit and now had experienced, first hand, God's power in his life.

With that bit of experienced knowledge he became so radical for Jesus. I never saw one like him. At first when he would go into the streets, Pastor John put him on my witness team. He thought everyone had a demon and he wanted to cast it out of them. I told Pastor John to get him off my team, I couldn't handle him. Pastor John said, "Fast and pray for him. God's going to train that boldness to be used in a mighty way for Him." So I did.

In a few short weeks Russell and I became great friends and I was able to teach him about deliverance and street witnessing. He and I would stay on Daytona Beach endless hours and into the late night hours just leading kids to Jesus. So many received Jesus. It was like a new anointing came on us, a boldness like I had never experienced.

The street kids, gang members and prostitutes learned to trust us as their friends. I remember one night one of the girl prostitutes came running looking for me. She was crying and said, "Mom, would you pray for me? I was raped, I feel so dirty." She would sell her body daily but a rape caused her to run to Jesus. Praise the Lord she knew where to come.

Never think the seed of the Gospel you sow falls on deaf ears.

Eight months had passed since those days of working with Russell on the beach and I was so happy he was the one God was bringing to me to walk the cross with.

Soon the doorbell rang and when I opened it there stood a slim young man, smiling. His new look shocked me for a moment, so I just stood there and stared at him. He was so clean cut, his hair was short and he looked like a young preacher. When I last saw him he had long hair, wore a headband and dressed in the latest street fashion.

"Well are you going to ask me in?" he asked. I stammered, "Yes, yes, of course, come on in. You just look so different." There was a gentle quietness about this old found friend. The rest of that day we spent in the Word and in prayer.

The next day I got a call from Ruthie Davis of Daytona Beach; she, too, had heard of this walk I was taking and she wanted to be a part. So I invited her to come over also. When she arrived it was late afternoon. We all decided to go to a Bible study that night. While there, Pastor Joe asked if he could pray for me and I said, "Sure." As he began praying he went down and laid hands on my feet, then on Russell's and prayed,

"And how shall they preach except they be sent? As it is written, how beautiful are the feet of them that preach the Gospel of peace, and bring glad tidings of good things" (Romans 10:15).

There we stood with tears just streaming down our faces. It was the confirmation we needed. Pastor Joe had never met me and didn't know what we were planning. He then went to Ruthie and prayed over her Nahum 1:15. It was with great joy that we drove home that night.

We felt we should leave for our starting point on Thursday afternoon, again forgetting what God said about leaving on Good Friday.

It was late Thursday afternoon and Russell and Ruthie still hadn't arrived from Daytona Beach. A dear friend of mine came to say good-bye. He saw the thin tennis shoes I was wearing and he said, "Are those the best shoes you have to wear?" I said, "Yes, but they are well broken in and they will be okay." He said, "No, they won't." So he took me shopping for the best Reebok walking shoes he could find.

By the time we got back Ruthie and Russell were there. We packed the car with one suitcase each, a couple of tents, towels, maps and some camping gear. We were tying the 12 x 6 cross to the top of the car when the phone rang. It was three of my friends who were waitresses. They said, "Don't leave until we get off work because we want to be a part of you ministry. We want to give you our tip money."

Praise the Lord! We had said, "Father, none of us have any money to take so You're going to have to provide all the way!" They didn't arrive until about 11:30 p.m. They gave us $75. We just stood there, praising God. There was our gas money we needed to get started. We said our good-byes, prayed together and jumped into the car.

Guess what time it was—12:30 a.m. Good Friday! We drove to our starting point near Jacksonville, Florida on Highway 17. We stopped at a weigh station to sleep. Russell took his bed roll and slept outside on the ground with all the bugs, while Ruthie and I nestled down in the car for a few hours of sweet sleep.

The Walk from Florida to Washington, D.C.

The first days of walking were so important for more than one reason. It was a great price to pay and it took determination to stick it out, because our bodies were screaming with pain, but God saw us through.

Day 1

It was 6:30 a.m. and it wasn't the sweet sound of an alarm clock awakening me, rather it was Russell rapping on the car window saying, "Open up, I'm getting all bit up!" The bugs had enjoyed their breakfast, feasting on Russell. We prayed for him and prepared to walk the cross.

I will never for a lifetime forget the next hours. The three of us stood there in a circle holding hands, committing ourselves and this walk into God's hands. We prayed protection over our lives and put on the whole armor of God. During the time we were praying the devil must have loosed every no-see-um (a biting bug) in Florida to chew us up! We were all so badly bitten. Even with all the bites, we had such a joy and excitement come upon us during these first few moments of the walk that would forever change our lives.

I remember those first miles as how I felt so much joy flooding my soul, that I could hardly contain it. At first, I began following Russell, carrying the wagon loaded with rain gear, tracts and water to drink, in the grassy area along side of the road. The grass made the wagon just too hard to pull. I decided to move up on the road to walk directly behind Russell.

I made a strap that went around my belly to pull the wagon, freeing up my hands to wave at the cars as they passed. I was walking along, smiling and waving at the cars as they passed by, and never realized what was happening to Russell.

Later, he told me that for a half hour or so, there was a real battle going on in his mind. The devil was telling him, "Look at you carrying that cross, walking with a lady pulling a little red wagon! You look like a fool! Just throw that cross in the ditch! Besides you are never going to make it to Washington; the cross is too heavy for you to carry."

Russell said he heard me saying, "Isn't this great, Russell?" He wanted to shout, "No!" but instead, he just prayed and asked the Father to help him.

Then the devil reminded Russell about all those bugs chewing us up, and he'd start itching until he thought he could not stand it anymore. It was during one of these mind battles when a medical supply truck came along. "Do you have need of any bug spray or sun block?" they asked. Russell told them how badly bitten we were by the bugs and they gave us something that immediately stopped the swelling and itching.

It was then that Russell regained control of things. New strength came and he began smiling and waving at the cars as they passed by.

The first six miles of walking were a snap. People were coming out of their homes, businesses, churches and stores to see the cross. We heard that one lady said to one of the store owners that she gave us food because she thought we could be angels. So many people would stop and talk to us. We had news coverage in those first few hours of walking. Children came out to the cross and wanted to walk with us.

As the day went along the 80-pound cross became very heavy on Russell's shoulders. At that time he only weighed about 145 pounds. My wagon was also becoming heavier and harder to pull. By this point our legs were hurting so badly, but we just prayed and kept pushing forward!

Russell had been a marathon runner and had much longer legs than I, so it was a constant push to keep up with him. We would walk four miles and rest for ten minutes. Towards the end of the day, we would rest five minutes after every two miles. I was very happy when people stopped to talk with us because it would not only give us a chance to minister to them, but it gave us a chance to rest. However, there was a price to pay for stopping because every time we started back up again, our legs would lock up and the pain would set in for five minutes or so.

On that first day I was introduced to another problem I had not thought about—what to do when there were no bathrooms for miles. Russell would use the woods, But I said, "I'll wait." That worked out as long as there were gas stations along the way, but there came a time when I had to go and there was no gas station in sight. Russell said, "Pick your bush."

I hate snakes, so I asked him to go into the bushes and check it out for me first. He checked it out and said that it was okay. I thought I went where he had checked it out, but I got all tangled up in a bush and got all scratched up. Russell just stood and laughed at me when I came out. Soon, I learned how to care for that matter myself.

When you walk, it is just you, the road and Jesus. We would spend hours in prayer and when we entered a city, or where someone would stop us, we would be so in tuned with the Holy Spirit that the Spirit of God would just move.

That very first day several people gave their lives to Jesus. All along the way people would bring us soft drinks and food. It was great. One car of grown men yelled out at Russell, "Jesus never had a wheel. Be a real man and carry that cross." Russell yelled back, "Here, you carry it!" They quickly took off.

It was about 4:00 in the afternoon and Russell said, "Lord, I can't carry this cross, it's just too heavy. You've got to help me." The Lord replied, "Can you carry it a few more miles?" Russell said, "Yes, Lord," thinking that someone was going to come out and rescue him from having to carry the cross. By this time, our legs were screaming in pain. But we had to keep going.

We soon walked into Woodbine, Georgia. Russell saw the empty streets and said, "Lord, I thought you were going to help me?" Just then I noticed a huge saw mill off the side of the road. I said, "Russell, look at that huge saw mill." Then the Holy Spirit told Russell, "Look, a saw mill with SAWS." Russell said, "Let's go over there because I'm going to get this cross cut down."

So we went over only to find the place closed. Russell said, "I just know there's got to be someone here." A few minutes later a large black man named Skeeter came out and asked if he could help us. Russell began telling him what we were doing and asked him if there was anyone who could cut the cross down. He said he would gladly do it for us.

He picked up that 80-pound cross like it was a toothpick. He took the wheel off and cut the main beam down, and then cross beam. He then had to re-drill holes to put the wheel back on. We were there for about an hour and found out he was a Christian. Normally he would have been gone he said, but he had a few things he thought he would do before leaving. Praise God, He kept Skeeter there for us! We asked him what we owed him and he said to keep on going down the road and tell others about Jesus. What a blessing!

As we walked through the town, again people came out to greet us. People were so hungry for Jesus. It was now early evening and our driver, Ruthie, came to pick us up. Ruthie marked our stopping point so we would know where to begin our walk the next day. We had walked 26 miles, and our bodies felt every mile.

We drove into New Brunswick, Georgia to the Salvation Army, which was where we had planned to spend our first night. When I tried to get out of the car, I could not move. My legs had locked up and my feet were full of blisters the size of half dollars. I heard Russell moaning in pain the same way I was.

Now, you would think after such an exciting day, there would be a group of people cheering us on. Not so. Instead, we were staying at the Salvation Army with people conducting police checks. We showed them who we were with our promotional materials and asked them to please call the Ocala Salvation Army, because they knew who we were. With that, we were allowed to spend the night.

We were exhausted and in tremendous pain. That night I prayed, "Father, we are all out here doing our best for You. Please, Father, I know this isn't Your best. Show us a better way to find lodging in better conditions, and I thank you, Father."

The night was filled with continual leg cramps, yet I awoke rested and ready for another great day.

Day 2

The second day on the road was filled with more pain, and it got worse. It hurt so badly I thought I would die, walking on blisters and with almost unbearable pain. There were long stretches of road with no cities along the way and very few people. The strong wind blowing against us made it hard to carry the cross and pull the wagon.

My wagon had the picture of The Bride attached about two feet above the back of the wagon which acted like a sail on a sail boat. Russell had battled with thoughts of quitting but God gave us the strength to continue. We continued to smile and wave as cars passed by but even that took all the energy we could muster. Russell and I spoke very little while walking. Most of the time was spent in communication with the Father.

While walking, the Lord had shown me how to obtain lodging. We sent Ruthie, our driver, who knew the route we were taking ahead of us, to obtain lodging for us from the local churches. This would be a large task but we prayed that God would give her wisdom and favor.

It was 6:00 p.m. and we had walked 27 miles, and there was no sign of Ruthie. So we contacted the local police department and sent them to find her. Forty-five minutes later they found her and told her to meet us at the major intersection in New Brunswick. There we stood with the police, the cross and wagon as she drove up to the intersection across the street. We felt relieved knowing comfort was in sight.

When the light turned green, she went on through the intersection, leaving us on the street corner. "How could she have missed us?" we asked. The police had to chase her down and bring her back to where we were. As we waited there, our legs had locked up, and the pain was so great we could hardly get into the car. Then she broke the news—we were scheduled to speak at a Full Gospel Business meeting.

New strength came as we hobbled our way to the meeting. We arrived in time to eat a wonderful steak dinner. I laugh thinking back to when they called us forward to speak. We both stood up and had to literally hold onto each other and the tables as we moved forward because of the great pain. Afterwards, we stayed the night in the home of Pastor Bill and Dorothy Ligon. It was simply beautiful. I felt like a queen, thanking Jesus for blessing us! Our God is an Awesome God!

Easter Sunday

Day 3

Early the next morning, Pastor Bill came out on the road to see us off. I will never forget how we all stood there praying and how the power of God fell on us.

Pastor Ligon said, with tears falling down his face, "Through all the pain and when every part of you bodies are crying out to quit, you keep on walking, pressing on, getting tough. Don't quit when you come to the end of yourself. Then God's great strength will carry you through. The prayer support as you walk will increase. It will strengthen you and you will see the power of God move through you, as you walk, talk to people, lay hands on people and pray with them."

With great confidence we began walking, smiling and waving at all the cars as they passed by. The morning went fairly well but by early afternoon the pain began again. The sun was beating down on us, draining our energy as the sweat poured off our bodies. We cried out, "Jesus! Help us! We must have Your supernatural strength. The Word says, what is impossible with man is possible with God, and it's only through You, Lord, that we can make it!"

This was our prayer over and over again.

God, in His goodness and mercy, sent us help. He sent a young engineer, Tom, along with his wife and son, to help us carry the cross and pull the wagon for about four miles. As Tom walked with the cross, he commented that, because of the weight of the cross and Russell's weight, that he would never be able to carry it all the way to Washington in the time frame we had allotted ourselves. However, he said he could design a bar with a wheel on it that would come up into the bottom portion of the cross beam which would hang down over Russell's shoulder and help take the weight off of his shoulder. This would allow him to push and guide the cross down the road. Excited about this prospect, Russell asked Tom how soon he could have it made. Tom said he could have it done the next day and he would meet us on the road. We praised the Lord for sending him our way.

This brought new hope for Russell and the spirit of quitting left him. We walked 27 miles that day and were so tired. Our bodies were racked in pain so badly that our sleep that night was again interrupted with leg cramps. We prayed again that night, "God, You must help us!"

The Glory of the Lord Came Down

Day 4

Pain, Pain, Pain, Pain! Other than for the pain, the early morning walk went better. But then came the rain.

We would get soaked, then we would dry, and then get soaking wet again. What a mess! Looking ahead, we could see the rain coming down in sheets. Thunder and lightning were everywhere. We were passing under a bridge and I suggested we rest under the bridge until the storm passed.

"Not a chance!" Russell said. "We've got to keep moving! This way to Washington, lady." In my mind, I thought, *This guy is nuts. Doesn't he know how dangerous this is?* Russell continued to walk, so I followed quoting Psalm 23. We were walking in water at times that almost covered our shoes. Thunder and lightning was striking all around us, and I was pulling a little metal wagon. I prayed, "Lord, protect us from this storm."

There were tall trees on both sides of the road, and it felt like they were watching the cross pass by. As the wind blew through their branches it was like they were applauding the cross as it passed by.

Then came another down pour, with heavy rain blurring our sight and soaking us through and through. I could not remember if there were any cars that passed by or not. It felt like I was all alone with Jesus, Russell and the trees. I began praising the Lord for His protection. Then, all of a sudden, I felt like I was a little girl splashing in the water without a care in the world. The cool water had a healing effect on the blisters on my feet. It felt great. We were walking side by side through the storm. I wanted to stay as close to the cross as I could.

I said, "Russell, do you feel that?" He said, "Yes, I can't even feel the weight of the cross. It's like I'm not even carrying it." My wagon was full of water from all the rain. It should have been twice as hard to pull. Yet, I too, couldn't feel the weight. The pain in our legs was gone. The rain soothed our badly sun-burned faces and arms.

At that moment, it was like Jesus was beside us, talking to us. We no longer noticed the storm. We were enjoying our fellowship with Him. It was glorious! This went on for a mile or so until the storm passed. We had been in the presence of Jesus Himself. He carried us through the storm. We stopped and lifted praises to Him thanking Him for His protection and the supernatural experience we had with Him.

Within a few miles, we were dried off and the pain was worse than I had ever felt. The heat was so scorching that our faces and arms were badly burned from the sun. It was like in the past four days every one of the elements was poured out on us to make us give up. But there was an inner strength that kept us going.

We had walked 29 miles and we had four more miles to go to the next town. Russell said that everything in him was screaming, "You can't make it!" But we could not stop here; we had to make it into the next town. We stopped and prayed, "Father, please help us!"

Just then a couple of guys pulled up in a pickup truck, and one of them said, "I'll carry that cross for you." "Great!" Russell said, as he handed him the cross. He took off like a race horse. Down the road and out of sight he went. We did not know if we would ever see him or the cross again.

Meanwhile, we both pulled the wagon into town, pushing our legs to keep on going. It was so hard. By the time we walked into the edge of town, we saw our driver, the man with the cross, and a newspaper man taking our picture. We were not walking and waving as normal, but rather holding each other up, dragging ourselves into town.

In all of these past four days there was some ministering. People were prayed for and some gave their lives to Jesus. There were hardships and many chances to quit, but if you keep on doing what God has told you to do, you will never be the same and you will see glorious victory and success in whatever you are doing. Too often people have a job to do, but they quit and give up and never realize the fullness of what a wonderful plan God has for them. *Never, never quit!*

The Cross Gets a New Wheel

Day 5

We had just begun our walk this day when Tom, the engineer we met a few days earlier, drove up and had the bar and wheel for the cross. Russell was so excited! Tom drilled a hole up into the cross beam and inserted the bar with the wheel on it, up into the cross beam. This allowed Russell to walk under the cross and push it down the road, getting the weight off his shoulders. Tom also placed a bolt into the bar which helped Russell to turn the wheel.

Russell felt like a new man. We began praising God for bringing Tom by our way to fix the cross, enabling Russell to walk the cross without the weight on his shoulder. This was great encouragement to Russell, however, it presented a real challenge for me. Remember the guy who took off with the cross like a race horse? Well, that is what Russell did.

By now his legs began to work easier, and his blisters were beginning to heal. Not so with me. This was my weakest day by far. I wanted to stop so many times because of the pain. Russell became a real pacesetter and pushed me along. At one point, I went into the restroom at a gas station and cried because of the pain. I said, "Father, why does this have to hurt so much?"

So softly He answered back and said, "You said you wanted to love Me in the same way Arthur Blessitt loved Me, but you can never realize this until you walk the same as he did." Then I remembered how Arthur, at times, could wring blood out of his socks when he first began. Or, how his shoulder would bleed from the weight of the cross. I had to get my eyes off the problem and on to why we were carrying the cross. It was because of my love for Jesus, so I had to keep focused.

Keeping up with Russell's long legs and his renewed pace was hard. Then the Father spoke to me and said, "The joy of the Lord is your strength." Another time He said, "So you want to be a general in My army? Then let's go...left, right, left, right! All good men will win this fight." I found if I *said*, "Left! Right!" whenever I fell behind Russell I could easily catch up. I soon thought of another way I could get him to stop. Whenever we stopped, I was the water girl. I would keep Russell well watered, thus causing more frequent stops. That became my secret weapon!

We passed by a girl in a wheel chair about 50 feet off the road. Walking at our speed, we simply waved to her and said, "Jesus Loves you." and we kept on walking. All of a sudden the Spirit of God came upon both of us and said, "I didn't call you out here to run a marathon, but to show My love to the people."

We quickly repented, and things began to change. People came running to the cross for prayer. Others came bearing food and some gave money! What a blessing because we were down to our last dollar. We had promised when we started that we would never ask for any money. If God was in this walk with us, He had to supply gas for the car, food, and lodging.

Earlier, I had told Russell we were down to a dollar and some change and that we could not even buy a soft drink or snacks. Russell asked, "Is that fear I hear coming out of your mouth? Who's your Father?" Those words rang over and over again in my mind: *Who's your Father?* I thought of the words in Matthew 6:25-33.

Therefore I say unto you, Take no thought for your life, what ye shall eat, or what ye shall drink; nor yet for your body, what ye shall put on. Is not the life more than meat, and the body than raiment?

Behold the fowls of the air: for they sow not, neither do they reap, nor gather into barns; yet your heavenly Father feedeth them. Are ye not much better than they?

Which of you by taking thought can add one cubit unto his stature?

And why take ye thought for raiment? Consider the lilies of the field, how they grow; they toil not, neither do they spin:

And yet I say unto you, That even Solomon in all his glory was not arrayed like one of these.

Wherefore, if God so clothe the grass of the field, which to day is, and tomorrow is cast into the oven, shall he not much more clothe you, O ye of little faith?

Therefore take no thought, saying, What shall we eat? or, What shall we drink? or, Wherewithal shall we be clothed?

(For after all these things do the Gentiles seek:) for your heavenly Father knoweth that ye have need of all these things.

But seek ye first the kingdom of God, and his righteousness; and all these things shall be added unto you.

On this day and the days that followed, I learned to know Him. He is my Jehovah-Jireh, my Provider. He is Jehovah-Rohi, my Shepherd and Protector. He is Jehovah Shalom, my peace, and He is Jehovah Rophe, my Healer. HE is everything I have need of!

This will become a greater revelation to you as you gain experiential knowledge of Him. Sitting in front of your television watching soap operas and junk TV only steals your time as well as your knowledge of God. Give God a chance to work in your life by stretching yourself to know Him in a more real way.

Day 6

This day brought more rain and strong winds, which seemed to work against us. The weather made walking very hard, but the pain in our legs was beginning to ease up a bit. During the past few days, our driver got lost numerous times. But this time it was us. We were walking on a four lane highway towards Savannah, Georgia and we could see Savannah up ahead and slightly off to the right of us.

The next thing we noticed, we were passing by Savannah which was now to the right and behind us. We had missed our road signs and ended up on a bypass around Savannah when we were supposed to be going into the city. So we stopped and got directions in order to get back on our road. This road took us miles out of the way, but God knew right where we were and He had a plan. What do you think the chances of two people walking a cross that both would miss the road signs? I believe our eyes were blinded to those signs.

As we went down this new road, many people came out to the cross, many bringing drinks and food for us. Many of these people ministered to us in a special way.

Then we heard someone shout, "Jesus never had a wheel. Be a real man and carry the cross!" As we looked around, we saw that quite a crowd of people beside a house were having a cookout and family gathering. Russell motioned for them to come out to the cross and they all came. We laughed and talked with them. We told them of our pilgrimage to Washington, D.C. and about Jesus.

This was a good Italian family, and before we left, they had all repeated the sinner's prayer. When we were about to leave, they loaded us up with food, and water, and the Godfather, as I called him, took off his hat and went around to each of them in the group and had them put money into the hat. If he felt they should put more in, he would shake his hat. We told them the Gospel was free and that they did not have to pay for it. But he insisted, saying, "You don't understand. We want you to be able to keep going down this road and telling others about Jesus the way you told us." Praise God!

We had quite a long way to go to reach the road we were supposed to be on and it was getting late in the afternoon. So we walked and walked, taking little time for rest. We had walked 31 miles this day. By the time we got to our highway, it was early evening. Ruthie, our driver, had thought something happened to us and was glad to find us.

Day 7

What a wonderful day! Russell was pushing the pace hard, but now I was able to keep up with him. I love walking in the early morning hours. You hear sounds you have never heard before, as all creation is praising God. The wind brings a beautiful smell as it blows across the fields. It seems as though all your senses have just awakened and you become more aware of everything.

As you walk along those lonely stretches of road, you keep in constant praise and communication with the Father. The animals in the fields notice you as the cross passes by. They stand at attention and watch. You can almost hear them say, "There goes the cross." You may laugh but it is the truth. Then as you approach the cities, tired in body and racked in pain, you feel renewed energy coming over you.

We waved and smiled at hundreds of cars as they passed by us. Some people honked and showed thumbs up; others told us to get a real job. Many people mocked us, and many shouted, "Jesus never had a wheel!" Yet so many other people had so many questions.

People are so hungry for Jesus. I liked walking through the black communities because they are so receptive to the cross. While walking through the country, we came across a wonderful Georgia plantation home. Some family members came out to the cross and asked us to go inside and pray for their mother. What a blessed time that was.

After a while, I noticed that Russell seemed to be troubled over something. It was like a battle going on in his mind. I noticed then that he would not hug me anymore. He would hug Ruthie but always kept his distance from me. I could not understand why. I am a hugger and I always hug my children. Since Russell was young enough to be my son, I always felt that I could hug him. I felt a real bonding between the two of us. We were out on the road together and we depended on each other. There was a real spiritual tie forming as we began to flow in the Spirit as one.

When I asked him what was bothering him, he would not say. He told me that it was a personal thing and it was being handled. Years later I found out what it was. As we were walking, he was thinking about all we had been through so far and about the strength God had given me for a woman my age to be walking that pace. Then he began to think of how we witnessed together all those months in Daytona Beach and now, here we were. Then he heard, "One day, she'll be your wife." He said, "I rebuke you, Satan. No way!" That explained the coldness I was beginning to receive from him.

Day 8

This day we walked on Interstate 95. We had to have special permission to walk this 10-mile section. We were stopped by a policeman and he was so hard on us, saying that he was going to arrest us and fine us $100 each. We told him we had special permission, but he said he did not care, and we had to get off the interstate. Again, we told him what we were doing and this time I added, "This walk is being covered by every major news network. I'm surprised you haven't heard of us." With that, he said, "Oh," and gave us a police escort, which only drew more attention to the cross.

Praise God for His wisdom in giving me the right words to say. Thousands of cars passed us while we were carrying the cross and many of the people honked their horns. Without realizing it, every time we were in a situation when there were hundreds of people looking at the cross, honking their car horns as they passed by, we forgot about the pain and there was an energy that happened. Praise God! "Let everyone who sees the cross be convicted to make a decision for You today," I would say.

Again we were back on Highway 17, which is a long stretch of barren road, and Russell was pushing me harder than ever. I cried out, "Jesus, please slow Russell down. I can't take this pace." We had walked about 29 miles and a couple of car loads of people stopped us to talk. They said Watersboro was 17 miles away. That was going to be our stopping point. Then Ruthie came along and it was 5:00. Seeing how tired we were she tried to get us to quit. At this point, Russell was ready to stop for the night, but I felt like we needed to go two more miles. He said, "Yes, in fact I could do six miles." So we told Ruthie to drive ahead two more miles and we would see how we felt. I thought to myself, *He's crazy!*

But off we went, when in a short time, a drunk man drove up and stopped to talk to us. He was a nice man, however intoxicated, and I believe used of Satan to stop us from going on. He said whatever you do, do not go by Clyde Connors, an old slave trading place about two miles up the road. Bad things happen there, and people get knifed there continually. They had killed people there, so avoid it at all cost.

Russell and I both said, "Sounds like that's where we need to be." We immediately began praying in the Spirit and pulling down strong holds, taking authority over the situation and pleading the blood of Jesus over our lives. When we rounded the bend in the road, we could hardly believe our eyes. There must have been 50 to 70 people on the outside of this place, drinking and yelling. The majority of them were black. Ruthie had parked Russell's car right in front of this place. They all stared at us as we walked up.

So, to break the ice Russell said, "Okay, what did you do with the white lady?" referring to Ruthie. They replied, "Oh man, she's all right.

She's inside." So we propped up the cross, parked the wagon and went inside. There was Ruthie inside the bar with my picture of "The Bride" explaining the salvation message, talking at the top of her lungs over the noise of the crowd.

After seeing she was all right we went outside and began ministering one on one. Russell began preaching to those in front and at the side of the bar and I went across the street where I saw somewhere between 15 to 18 men under a tree drinking. I jumped up on a parked car and began to preach, telling them the Good News Gospel.

I explained they didn't have to wait until they quit drinking to receive Jesus; they could do it right now. I said to them, "If you want Jesus to change your life, come and stand here now." With that nine men put down their drinks, took off their hats and repeated the sinner's prayer. Russell had the same kind of results. What a time of revival we had there. Just think what we would have missed if we would have listened to the negative reports and gotten off the road sooner.

That night our host pastor came over and blessed us. We told him of the results we had and he said that they would minister and follow up in that area. Praise the Lord!

Day 9

More blisters, but our legs were getting stronger every day. We stopped by a Burger King to eat lunch. Russell went inside as I waited out by the cross. They were having a carnival behind the Burger King and when the kids saw the cross, I soon was surrounded by many inquiring minds. They consisted of cheerleaders, football players and other high school and junior high youngsters, all full of questions: "Where are you going? You really walked all that way? Why?" On and on it went.

I was able to tell them how Jesus changed my life. I spoke of His love for them and that He had a very special plan for their lives and that He was the friend who would never let them down. Before we left we were able to repeat the salvation prayer with them. Great seeds were planted into their hearts. They stood there and cheered us on as we walked.

Later, at a country store, Russell was able to minister to several country boys who bought us some snacks. We got so much news coverage, which I loved because, as people read the story, or watched us on TV, or heard us on the radio, they would be reminded to think about their relationship with Jesus.

Later, that afternoon, as we kept walking, a young man named David jumped out of a truck and walked with us. He wanted us to spend the night with his group. My spirit did not witness with him and the Father said, "Have nothing to do with this man." Later, we found out he was with an occult group who had a commune nearby. Praise God for His witness that keeps us.

When we would get up in the morning we would never know where our meals, gas or lodging were coming from. We always prayed over Ruthie and asked that she would have God's wisdom as she went seeking lodging. That night we were blessed to eat supper with the Methodist Church as they had a carry-in dinner. We still had problems with our legs locking up when we stopped walking. You would have laughed to see us holding onto the hand rails as we pulled ourselves up the numerous steps of the church. We were asked to speak and with our legs locking up and needing help to walk, you would wonder how we ever walked all those miles.

Day 10–15

Several years ago, we were visiting a television station in Louisiana during a time when they had a flood. My diary of this walk was five feet under water, so I lost many of the notes that happened on those days.

However, I remembered we were averaging about 24 miles a day. The winds were cold and quite bad and our toes were numb from the cold. We were receiving a lot of news coverage and, because we did not act as some Jesus freaks out there, but were real with the news people, they did great stories. We were able to plant good seed in them. One newsman gave his heart to Jesus and came back out to see us several times.

People were still stopping and bringing us food, snacks and drinks as we were walking, encouraging us to go on. It was all Jesus, providing just what we needed for that day. We have been blessed with great lodging, homes or motel rooms, daily, just as He said that first night!

Russell was still walking so fast it was hard to keep up. I continually prayed for help, or that somehow, he would realize he had to slow down for me. He was such a pace setter on the long stretches, I would pray for people to stop so I could rest.

For days we would wave at the many logging trucks as they passed by. They would continually honk at us, waving and giving us a thumbs up. One day, one of the truckers stopped and asked why we were walking so far. We told him about Jesus and he received Christ that day as his Savior. We saw so many salvations.

The word of the cross coming down the road spread and people would wait out on their porches or line the road to see us as we passed. We never knew what the next bend in the road would bring.

As we were walking a lonely road in Georgia, there was a large chain gang of approximately 25 to 30 men. You can imagine it raised quite a stir as we came into their midst. We found favor with the guards and they let us witness to them and pass out tracts, however, we were not allowed to spend a lot time with them.

Later that afternoon, we passed them again up by the bridge they were working on. This time, we got them all in a circle, holding hands, repeating the sinner's prayer. This very much disturbed one of the guards who told us we had to move on. So we prayed for God to cover and protect the seed sown and that He would bring others by their paths to teach them and raise them up in the Word.

We passed a road crew and were able to share Jesus with them. As we walked on, I kept seeing in my mind's eye those orange jackets they were wearing. When we stopped for our break, I said, "Russell, I'd love to have orange jackets like those road workers had. That way people could better see us walking and we could write signs on them."

So we joined hands, prayed and agreed for them according to Matthew 18:19 where it says that if two agree as touching anything that they ask, it shall be done for them by God the Father.

We did this kind of praying daily. Within a half an hour those road workers came by, handed us two of those orange jackets and said the Georgia Highway Department would like us to wear them while we were walking. We said, "Praise the Lord! We just prayed for them."

That night I took a black magic marker and wrote on the back of my jacket in black letters "JESUS LOVES YOU" and on Russell's, "WHEN ALL ELSE FAILS TURN ON TO JESUS—HE NEVER FAILS." This made us an even greater witness as we walked. These jackets also were a blessing because now we could walk on any secondary highway in America. Praise the Lord!

The mile markers on the sides of the road were very important to us. It may seem silly to you but they are great pace setters. We walked a whole day without them and it was a hard walk.

Jesus knows our every need. He sent a street preacher by the name of James, who was on his way to Washington, to help us. It was cold and windy the day he stopped to talk to us. He had a converted van with a kitchen, so he invited us to come in and get warm because we were freezing. He made us hot chocolate and soup. Soon we were warm; then he asked if there was anything he could do for us. Russell said, "We need mile markers every two or four miles."

He said, "No problem," as he pulled out a roll of orange fluorescent ribbon. "I'll go ahead and mark all the miles for you."

Praise the Lord! What a major blessing he was to us. As we walked, we realized it is the small things that mean so much. God is always there meeting our every need.

It was wonderful. No television, only Jesus, the road and the people. So many hungry faces, lost and searching for that peace that only Jesus can give. We walked through the most beautiful city. It was Manning, South Carolina, a city whose streets were lined with pine trees and white dogwoods. Azaleas were in full bloom as were many spring flowers. The lawns were manicured and surrounded with a beauty of color. Wisteria hung from the trees which made it simply breathtaking. It was a great time to remind ourselves of the beauty God created.

The Night the Cross Spent in the Bar

The next day, we had a television interview, but it was a little different from the others. The newsman from the local CBS station came while we were ministering. One man gave his life to Jesus. It made me think of the time the blind man in the Bible said, *"One thing I know, that, whereas I was blind, now I see"* (John 9:25). So it was with that man, who accepted Jesus and had such a joy on his face. What a great testimony of God's live to be shown on television.

It was late afternoon and Ruthie came to us and said, "All I can find for accommodation is the floor of a church. What do you think?" My spirit rose up within me and I said, "No way! We are out here doing our best for Jesus and that is not His best." We needed to shower and soak our legs. "No, that won't do."

Needless to say, she was a little upset with me. She had tried to find something all day and now here I was sending her out again. We prayed with her to have God's wisdom and off she went. You see, we could have accepted that, but just listen to what we would have missed.

It was about 6:30, and still, no Ruthie. We were very tired as we had walked many miles that day. We walked into Sellers, South Carolina that Friday night. Many people were already gathering around a local bar. They stopped us and asked us what we were doing with that cross. "Were we with the KKK?" they asked. Questions and more questions.

So we decided to have a street meeting right there, and we began to praise the Lord with singing. Then Russell preached the Good News Gospel. A black girl, named Barb, interrupted and yelled at Russell, and he said back to her, "Have you asked Jesus into your heart?" She said, "Yes, I have." Then he said, "Have you been baptized in the Holy Ghost?" She said, "No, and I don't want your Holy Ghost."

Russell continued to minister and many gave their lives to Jesus. It was wonderful! Afterwards, he was talking to some of the people. Just then, James drove up and opened the side door to his van. Being tired and having blisters, I sat down in the doorway of the van. Soon I was surrounded by lots of children, two years to 14 years old. They asked, "Did you really walk all that way?" I showed them the blisters on my feet. Then I began to talk to them about Jesus, and how much He loved them. They all said the Salvation prayer with me.

Then, the strangest thing happened. Mothers were putting their babies into my lap, and with tears running down my face, I began praying prophetic prayers over each of them. Then, the children lined up and wanted me to lay hands on them and pray for each of them. Again, I prayed prophetically. That had never happened to me before; it was all by the Spirit of God.

What happened next is almost unbelievable. Barb, the girl who yelled out at Russell, said, "I've been standing here watching what's happening and it's real. I want it." So we prayed the Salvation prayer and she asked to be baptized in the Holy Spirit. What a miracle, what a change, what a real revival! Her mother, Gertrude, owned the bar and she asked us to come in and eat. I will never forget those precious children in the bar, watching us as we ate. What a time we had!

By then it was dark, about 9:30, and still no Ruthie. We asked James if he would mind driving ahead and seeing if he could find her. We stayed there in the bar with our new found friends continuing to minister. Our pains were gone and it seemed as though we had a new strength.

It was about 10:00 p.m. when Ruthie and James returned and she said that she had met a wonderful Full Gospel Businessman and he wanted to take us out to tea. Gertrude, the lady who owned the bar, asked if she could keep the cross in the bar overnight, because she was so happy with the difference the cross had made, so we quickly agreed.

It was about 10:30 when we met the Full Gospel Businessman and his friend at the restaurant. They were so taken by our story and of what Jesus was doing that they wanted to be a real part. Not only did they bless us with food and money but they provided us a room at the Holiday Inn. When we arrived at the room, it was very late.

We were in our prayer time when the phone rang. It was the *700 Club*. That wonderful man who was our host that night had called his friend, a representative with the *700 Club* and told him our story. They interviewed me that night on the phone and said they wanted to be a part of our ministry. From that day forward, they, along with Full Gospel Businessmen, helped us find lodging in most of the cities.

Just think, if we would have settled for the floor of a church, what we would have missed.

Day 16

The next morning when we arrived back at the bar to begin our walk, we were so surprised to be welcomed by a crowd of people. There was Barb, Gertrude, a pastor from Philadelphia and so many others that we had met the night before, to say good-bye. We had a time of prayer and praise. They had taken an offering for us and begged us to come back some time. "Lord Jesus, how You blessed us." This was all a result of the many prayers that had been going with us. Praise the Lord for what He had done! I thought my heart would burst as we walked away after such a shower of love.

We were walking in such a strong anointing. All day long people came to the cross, accepting Jesus. When we stopped at McDonald's in Dillon, South Carolina, eight to ten girls ranging in age from 16 to 18, received Jesus. Russell had gone into the restaurant to get a soft drink and by the time he came out, the cross was surrounded with people.

Money came from everywhere, blessings upon blessings. I cried out as we were walking, "Father, thank you for your anointing and for allowing me to be used in this way. You are truly an awesome God. I love you so much." His praises were continually on my lips. Of all the things in the world I have done nothing could compare to this. The greatest joy one can have is seeing someone come to Jesus. I promise you, there is nothing like it!

Day 17

It was a beautiful Sunday morning. Our walk began near South of the Border, the hotel and attraction near Dillon, South Carolina. There were some beer cans thrown at us, but none hit us. He gives His angels charge over us so we know we have his protection.

We had walked up to a convenience store where a man, about 50 years old, stopped to talk with us. He bought us lunch and we continued to talk with him. He said his wife had been a Christian for many years, but he always ran from God. He did not have time for Him. We told him that it was because of her prayers for him that we were there now. With tears in his eyes, he accepted Jesus. He asked us to pray for his son who was in prison for drugs. He said he had to hurry and get to church to be with his wife. "Thank you, Jesus!" What more can one say?

There was a demon possessed man who came out to see us that same day. He spoke the Word but we recognized the demons in him. We took authority over them and commanded them, in the name of Jesus, to be still and leave. The devil will send deterrents to keep people from receiving Jesus, but the name of Jesus is above everything and the devil will have to be silenced!

It was a beautiful day with Jesus. On a long stretch of road we came upon a beautiful North Carolina home where we were invited to come in for refreshments. We visited at great length with a sweet grandmother and her daughters. She sat and wept as we prayed with her.

Sometimes when the wind blows so strong, the cross cuts into Russell's neck and shoulder area. This little grandmother wanted to bless us so she gave Russell a little pillow he could put on his shoulder to keep the cross from hurting his neck. Just another example of how God knew of our needs and provided for them.

Many people heard of the cross coming down the road, and drove miles to talk to us and have us pray for them. It was not us though. It was the cross. If we just walked down the road, would anyone notice? The cross is our fishing pole and the people are the fish we catch by the prompting of the Holy Spirit.

Day 18

When you have three people living so close together day in and day out, it truly takes the grace of God. The littlest things could become annoying and this day was such a day. It seemed as if we were all at each other's throats. We had walked in such a strong anointing for days, yet this day seemed as if everything led to an argument. What went wrong?

We had walked out of our way so we could walk the cross through a heavily depressed area. We asked the Father to forgive our striving and let the light of the cross shine so brightly. There was ministry, but privately, there was still this argumentative spirit. We were covered by a lot of news media in this area, again all of them giving us a great report.

We had just walked through St. Paul, North Carolina. The temperature was 75 degrees, but within minutes it dropped to 36 degrees. It was awful, the heavy rains and strong winds came. Russell and I held onto a telephone pole as tightly as we could while the winds and the rains whipped against us. Things were flying around but nothing hit us. At one point, the wind completely took our breath away! We then went up behind a mobile home to get out of the wind. We were freezing!

After about 45 minutes, it was still pouring rain, but the wind was not as bad. We walked over to a grocery store to warm up, because we were drenched. While in the store, we witnessed and led two girls to Jesus. Later, we heard a small tornado had hit. Praise God for His protection! It was after that storm that true repentance came. We asked the Father to forgive us and help us through these harder times and to help us to live at peace with one another. After this, a peace came and the heaviness was lifted, as once again, God blessed us in every way.

Day 19

Walking was wonderful. It was like you get up, turn on the key and your legs just go. The pains were gone. Praise the Lord!

We stopped by a country store this morning to get something to drink. I was able to pray with a Christian lady regarding her having a baby and for her marriage to be healed. When I came outside, Russell was up on the roof of the house next to the store, helping three black men put up an antenna. It was great how he was able to witness Jesus to them. When they wanted to pay him for his help, he said, "No. This one's on Jesus."

Preaching Jesus, along with showing His love, touched people in ways that they will never be the same.

It was those times like walking down those long stretches that the Lord really taught me. This day, He spoke so clearly to me about learning to rest in Him, which is having complete trust in Him for everything. Then He began speaking about the words of our mouths and how powerful our words were. It was a great time of fellowship with the Father. How I treasure those times of refreshing.

We were asked to minister on the radio by the *700 Club*. That night, we were blessed by meeting Ray Hill, one of the directors of the *700 Club*.

Day 20

Ray Hill, a director of the *700 Club* whom we met the previous day, asked if we could have lunch and meet with the Fayetteville, North Carolina pastors. It was a great experience, as they all laid hands on us and prayed over us.

The *700 Club* was such a blessing to us. They gave our car an oil change. Russell had a wisdom tooth that had been hurting him, so they sent him to a dentist who pulled his wisdom tooth and fixed several small cavities. They gave us as many tracts as we could use. They also gave us motel rooms *and* meals. We lacked for nothing! *"The Lord is my shepherd, I shall not want."* (Psalm 23:1)

Day 21

We won people to Jesus all day long. The anointing was so strong on Russell that day. At one point, he was praying over a large man and he fell out, right on the side walk. The man was instantly healed. Russell was praying over two other businessmen when the NBC TV Nightly News came over and taped a great story. They got shots of us ministering in the streets. They saw the power of God move as the man got up and told of his miraculous healing. Praise the Lord! The newspaper also gave us great coverage. I love it when the news covers the Good News story of the cross, because the witness of Jesus was not just on the road. It traveled throughout the entire area. Later that day, the man who was healed brought lunch out to us. He even had me take off my shoes and rubbed my tired feet. He was so happy to be healed.

At 4:00 that morning, I was suddenly awakened. The Lord spoke to me many things. He said, "Even this day will I set a standard before you that you will know that I, the Lord, your God, hath delivered you from the snare of the devil." At that time I was not sure what He meant, but all day long I was aware that God was going to show Himself mighty on our behalf.

It was getting to be late afternoon and we were on one of those long, lonely roads. Both of us, being very tired and knowing we still had eight miles or so to go, decided to stop and pray. We said, "Lord, we're so tired. Could you please just translate us to the next city?" When we opened our eyes we were still where we had been. We smiled at each other and kept on walking.

Within about fifteen minutes of that time, a jet black velvet car came from nowhere, it was just there. When it passed us, a cold chill came over me. My tongue got so fat I could hardly speak. Russell felt the same thing. In my spirit I knew the car would be coming back.

We were about to walk up this pretty steep hill when I began pleading the blood of Jesus over our lives, loosing the angels to do battle, binding up the works of the devil and called on the name of Jesus.

Soon we heard the car's tires squeal as the driver turned his car around and passed us. The car went up the hill and turned around, again coming down the hill straight at us. I yelled at Russell, "Stand and see the salvation of the Lord." Thinking the Lord was going to translate us, as we had prayed, we stood there. But instead, just before it got to us, the car swerved and went around us. I do not know who the driver was, but the coldness was gone and peace came.

We just praised God for His deliverance! He did just as He told me earlier that morning. When you experience Him speaking to you and seeing it happen, you will never be the same. It really builds your faith level.

When we walked into the city of Godwin, we were met by people from Heritage College and were asked to minister to their faculty and students. There was an instructor who had a wonderful story of how she had been healed from cancer. When she was told she had cancer, they said she only had a short time to live.

She did not choose to believe that report but chose to believe what the Word had to say about her situation. For seven months, every morning at 7:00, she would get up and remind the devil what the Word had to say about her healing. Then, she would put God in remembrance of His word, believing all the time for her healing.

One day, she told her husband that she was applying for a teaching job. He said that she was too weak and could not do it. She replied, "The Lord will help me." When she was in the elevator on her way to the job interview, she collapsed. She called on the name of Jesus to help her and she got the job! As she went to tell her husband her good news, a warm feeling went all over her. She was totally healed! Praise the Lord! She was such a blessing to me!

Day 22

Today, I believe we met the devil himself, face to face. As we were walking, we came upon a new pickup truck. Inside was a man, very nicely dressed in a black suit. He had piercing eyes, and several gold teeth glimmered when he smiled with that sinister smile he had. He yelled out at us. Russell said, "Dorothy, stay here. Something is not right."

We were within speaking distance of the man in the truck when he said. "You are wrong in what you are doing." He knew the Word but used it against us and what we were doing. He said we were not married and it was a bad witness for us out there with the cross, and he kept on putting condemnation and guilt on us, appealing to the flesh, not our spirit. Russell told him in the name of Jesus to be still and told him how we must obey God and not men. With that, we left as he sat there watching us. Then I turned around again, and he was gone. I am sure he was, either the devil or a messenger of Satan, sent to get us off the road.

It was early afternoon and we were walking through a small town in North Carolina. You could feel the heaviness as you walked through this town. We only saw a few churches, so I began to pray in the Spirit, knowing something just was not right here. There were a few cars that passed us with people yelling comments on how Satan rules. That, by the way, never bothers us because we immediately pray for those people and ask God to move by the Holy Spirit to bring Godly people across their paths to lead them to Jesus.

As we came out of the town, we were about to cross a bridge when we were surrounded by three police cars and six armed policemen. One was the police chief dressed in full uniform. Immediately I took over speaking with him and found out that they wanted to arrest us.

The Spirit of God gave me wisdom and I said, "I'm surprised you haven't heard about us. This walk is being covered by every major news network, ABC, CBS, NBC, and CNN, along with different radio stations and newspapers." With this I pulled out some of the articles written about us. He got very nervous and said, "You should have let us know because we would have rolled out the red carpet. Just be careful as you go down the road." Thank you, Jesus, for giving us your wisdom!

That became our weapon from that day forward when we had to deal with the police. They didn't want to be covered by the news in a negative way. We have been blessed to have such positive news reports by all the networks and papers. It's the favor of God!

By the way, all the time I was talking to the police chief, Russell was busy asking one of the other policemen if he had made Jesus his Lord. Later that day, another policeman stopped to talk with us. He asked if we had any trouble walking through the town where we had stopped. We told him what happened and he said, "Only God brought you through there, because the police force in that town are Satan worshippers."

Praise God for His protection! We began bombarding that city with prayer. It was after this that more people came out to the cross, such as a lady named Josephine who was healed and her husband who gave his life to Jesus.

Again, our host was Heritage College. Ruthie and I had the same room. I had just fallen asleep when she work me up and said she believed that Russell was beginning to fall in love with me, and I with him. I assured her that nothing could be further from the truth. He was like one of my sons. Impossible! I began to pray, "Father, please keep our hearts pure. Please help us, Jesus, to only keep our eyes on You and the work You have called us to do. I love you, Father."

Ever since she planted that seed, I was not able to get it off my mind. The thought about Russell would come and I would cast it down with the Word.

Day 23

Ministry was so great on the street this day. People of all walks of life were flocking to the cross. I have seen Russell growing so much in the Lord as he ministered and taught the Word. He prayed for a hernia and instantly it was healed. We were seeing miracles daily!

I was again bombarded with the thought of Russell. I continued to pray, "Lord, please help me to control my feelings. I must not allow myself to feel for this young man in any way." It just wouldn't work. It was a battle to keep focused on Jesus.

Again, this day was so hot the sweat was pouring off of us. Our sun burned faces and arms got worse. The sun seemed to sap all our energy, yet as people would come to the cross a refreshing came and we were able to go on.

Days 24, 25

Most of the healings we had up until this point were confirmed by the mouths of the people and not seen.

It was quitting time and Russell was very tired. We were putting the cross on top of the car when a man and his wife stopped us for prayer. He said he has seen us walking earlier that morning and prayed if he would see us on his way home then he would know God wanted us to pray for him. He proceeded to show us the lump on this chest; it stuck out perhaps three to four inches. He had been in a car accident ten years prior and as a result had a hiatal hernia. All of his food had to be mashed and he always had to sleep on his back. There were many foods he could not eat as they would make him sick.

So we gathered around him to pray and when Russell laid hands on his chest, without saying a word, the healing power of God totally healed the man. The lump went away, Russell felt it go. It shook Russell, so he said, "Did you see that?! It just went away!" He was so excited he kept going on and on. We just all stood there praising God for what He had done.

The night after the miracle, we stayed in the home of this man. He ate regular food for dinner and sausage for breakfast. He was so happy. The next three days that followed the man would drive up and say, "I'm still healed. Can I get you anything, anything at all?" Praise God.

Day 26

Pastor Allen, who was our wonderful host, walked the cross with us. He was the first pastor to do so. I noticed how it affected his life in such a real way!

Walking the cross does change a person. I cannot explain it. It gives a new boldness to ministry and the things that seemed so important do not have the same meaning any more.

All that matters is lifting up the name of Jesus and sharing Him with others. People and changed lives through Jesus are all that matter.

As we were walking, we met a lady who needed healing in her legs because they were very badly swollen. Some people brought her out to us. We stopped under this bridge to pray for her. Russell and I both knelt down and laid hands on her feet. While we were doing this, an ambulance came by and stopped. The drivers stood out by the ambulance while we prayed. They were both Christians and prayed with us. Praise the Lord, the lady was instantly healed.

I noticed Russell was starting to really slow down in his walk and took more rests on the long stretches.

Day 27

We only walked about 16 miles this day. Russell just could not go any more and the rest stops were getting longer and longer. His weight had gone down to 125 pounds. He needed rest.

We walked into Infield, North Carolina and there were a lot of drunks around the outside of a bar. We ministered to this drunk girl who kept yelling out at us. We watched as God instantly sobered her up. Immediately she went and got her other friends and made them sit and listen to her as she read them the salvation tract we gave her.

She said, "This is real. Look at me. Jesus sobered me up. I've given my life to Him, you have to do it too." Others got sobered and they, too, gave their lives to Jesus. You will never experience these kinds of things until you go out where the sinners are and show them the light of Jesus. It's great!

Day 28

We were to do a taped interview for the *700 Club* in Washington, D.C. at the Washington for Jesus festival. So we drove to Washington. It was very cold and rainy there but thousands of people were present. We taped with the *700 Club* standing there in the bitter rain and cold. All afternoon we were speaking to one newsman after another. I was losing my voice and Russell was very weak. The *700 Club* put us in the home of *Phil & Jackie Riley* who had become great friends of this ministry. What a blessing they were at Washington for Jesus.

Day 29

We walked the cross through the crowds. Again, witnessing to so many newsmen from around the world as they covered our story. Every network covered us. We were photographed all day long—many pictures. Again, we were interviewed by the *700 Club*.

In the morning's *Washington Post*, Russell and I were at the top of the front page in a picture that was at least 8 x 11 or so, along with our story. There were two other smaller pictures under ours talking about "Washington for Jesus." Only God could do such a thing.

This was a hard day for both Russell and me. His eyes seemed sunk back in his head. I could tell he was ill and very tired. The periodic rain and bitter cold didn't help much. By that evening when we went back to the Riley's home I had lost my voice and was running a high fever. We needed rest, as we had been walking now for 29 days straight with no rest.

Days 30–35

We went to Evangel Temple in Washington, D.C. and then back to the Riley's to rest. Russell looked very bad. By that time, Jackie felt as though we needed to take him to the hospital. On the way to the hospital we prayed for favor as we did not have any insurance. Immediately when they saw Russell, they admitted him and began running tests on him.

The doctor told us it was good we brought him in as his blood sugar was up to over 800 and we could have lost him. They would not let us see him that night. The next day, we were told he had sugar diabetes and would have to stay in the hospital for some time. They felt like walking the cross was completely out of the picture for him for a very long time.

This was a bad report and just did not fit into the plans of what God told us to do. We had to finish the walk from the Virginia border, where we left off, to Washington. How were we to do this with Russell in the hospital? We began praying, but ultimately it would have to be Russell's decision without any input from us.

While we were walking, God met every need we had, one day at a time and just in time. However, my bills at home were mounting up and my house payment was beginning to fall behind. I also needed money to pay the tuition for Tammy who was in school at RHEMA.

The pressure began to mount until one morning, Jackie, who was such a God-send, prayed with me and I just released it all to Jesus. I had to be willing to give up my home if that was what He required of me. That was hard, because I loved my home. It was where I raised the children and where we lived for 21 years. It was a struggle but when I released it to Him, a peace came.

Russell's spirit seemed to do great! When I went to visit him, he would say, "I cannot seem to get this doctor to understand that he has to release me because I know Jesus heals and '*By His stripes I am healed.*' Would you tell him?" Friday morning came and Russell said, "That's it. Either God and His healing power is real and it's for everyone or it's not. I'm checking out!" I quickly responded, "The doctor and nurse said you can't or you will die." He said, "Jesus has healed me!" So he signed himself out.

We packed up and drove back to the North Carolina, Virginia border. We prayed for Russell for strength. He said, "Dorothy, if I should die, you call me back in Jesus' name, because I'll be up there calling Him a liar because His Word says I'm healed."

Now you must remember Russell had been on insulin for five days to regulate him and to stop cold turkey is very dangerous; yet this was his decision. When we began walking, he was white as a sheet and the cross would sway as he carried it. I would pray, "God we need a miracle." We stopped to rest for about ten minutes then Russell said, "I need just a few more minutes." Another ten minutes passed and we prayed for strength for Russell and walked some more. Ruthie drove up and brought some juice for Russell.

While we were stopped, a black preacher from Washington, D.C. came out from his home which we had just passed to talk with us. He said God sent him home early from Washington, D.C. and just drove passed us and he pulled his car into the driveway. God told him he was to minister to us.

Then Russell, all pale and weak, said, "I believe you are to lay hands on me and pray for my healing." He agreed. Just like that the color came back into Russell's face and he began to dance around with the cross. He said, "I'm healed, I'm healed! Praise the Lord!" New strength came to Russell as we walked. God is so great!

As we walked on, we walked into a town that seemed very cold to the cross. It was as though all eyes were watching us but no one was responding to the cross. Then one black lady stopped and asked if we were with the KKK. We told her we were carrying the cross for Jesus. We told them how much He loves them and that it did not matter what color they were. It was like a loud speaker sounded what we were doing. In a short time the ice was broken and many came to the cross for prayer. There was a lot of ministering that took place.

Afterwards we learned that the weekend before we were there, the KKK paraded the streets, burning crosses. You can understand the apprehension in the community.

That night, we ministered in a church in Roanoke Rapids. It was great! Then the pastor prophesied over us and said Satan was setting a trap for us and to beware. I thought it was those thoughts and feelings I had for Russell so that really helped me to cast them down.

As we walked into Roanoke, Virginia, we met a wonderful businessman. He asked us not to use his name for the reason you will see later. He took us to supper and gave us a motel room to spend the night. We spent a lot of time ministering to him and sharing all the things God had done in our lives. He asked if he could walk the cross with us the next day. Of course we agreed!

He picked us up and took us to breakfast and we walked, praying with people and getting people saved. At one point a church group joined us and walked with us. We had one of the little girls pray for a girl we met on the street. That girl gave her life to Jesus. You will never know the great impact that had on that little girl's life. She will never forget that moment.

That night, our businessman friend again put us up in a motel and fed us. He had made arrangements for us to minister to the youth at a large church. God really moved in that service as many young people committed their lives to Jesus in a greater way.

That night when our friend took us back to the motel, he pulled out a note from his pocket. It was a suicide note. He was going to commit suicide and kill his wife and son, but God had other plans and brought an old wooden cross down the road to show him His love. Praise God! That was worth everything.

The next morning when I went out to the car, I met a Catholic priest there. He asked me about the cross and what we were doing with it. I told him our story and invited him to come to our room. He brought two of his traveling companions along. We sat and talked about everything that God has done.

He asked Russell to pray for his arm as he could not lift it up. So we prayed and Russell took his arm and lifted it above the priest's head. The priest began to cry. Russell told him to do it and he lifted it without any pain. He said, "I never knew Jesus in this way before. Thank you, thank you for sharing with me. It will change everything." Praise God!!

That day while we were walking, Russell had a blow out on the sole of his shoe. He took my hand and we prayed. He said, "Lord, my sock is showing. I need a new pair of shoes and I really need one size bigger because my feet are swelling." Shortly after that prayer, our businessman friend came by and he said he had just bought some shoes for himself and had never worn them and wondered if Russell could use them. They were a $100 pair of Rockport walking shoes, one size bigger than Russell needed, which was just what we had prayed for earlier. The Father never ceases to amaze me. When you walk with Him like this, day after day you learn to know His ways.

One day, we walked for about 15 miles on the frontage road to I-95. It was wonderful as hundreds of people waved and honked their horns at us. I got so high you would have thought I was drunk. Those people did not know us, but they are waving at the cross. How it must bless the Father.

Another day as we walked the cross on a lonely road, a man drove off of I-95 and said the Lord told him to get off the road and drive down Highway 301 and there we were. He opened up his trunk and had a newspaper picture of us from Florence, South Carolina. On this particular day you could not see us from I-95. At first, I thought maybe he was an angel, but when he prophesied over us I felt something strange.

He said, "What God had put together let no man put asunder." Repeatedly he told Russell he was going to be a pastor and that we would minister together as husband and wife. When we got to Washington, we would receive a large check. We would buy ourselves a house, etc. Again, he said, "What God has put together."

Russell began to jump for joy and shout. I did not know why he was so excited, if it was because of the thought of being pastor or what. Just hours before, he was telling me he wanted to go to Peru as a missionary and marry a beautiful dark skinned, long black hair girl. That sure did not fit what this man was saying.

Then Russell spoke up and said we were not married. The man said that God showed him things we hadn't seen yet and that God had married us in the Spirit and we would be married in the flesh. Then he said, "God uses the foolish things to confound the wise." I thought to myself this would surely be a foolish thing; this must be the trap of the devil that the pastor prophesied over us. When the man left, I said, "Russell, don't believe him. He must be a false prophet."

The walking in Virginia was beautiful. There were many killer hills though. Our legs once again were tiring. There was a lot of ministry and we were asked to preach in more and more churches. There were many late nights with little rest because of so much ministry. Praise the Lord!

The traffic was really heavy. I could feel the wind of the trucks as they passed by. We would have to remember, in the high traffic areas, to always wave with our right hand and not the left as we could lose an arm with the closeness of the traffic. Thank you, Father, for Your angels.

Salvations were too numerous to count. People were getting saved by the car loads. It was late evening and a car stopped us and asked what we were doing, as did so many others. There was an old black man sitting in the passenger seat who had never received Jesus. After ministering Jesus' love to him, he sat there with tears coming out of his eyes which turned crystal blue as he received Jesus for the first time. We all stood and wept.

Day after day, we were seeing God move in such mighty ways. A man driving a truck passed us and came back because he was wondering what we were doing. He gave his life to Jesus. His arm was in a sling, but when he prayed the sinner's prayer, his arm was instantly healed. Praise the Lord!

One night we stayed in a motel room provided for us by the Full Gospel Businessmen. While there, Ruthie made many calls ahead trying to line up our lodging. The next morning when I went down to the office to pray for the calls, the bill was $31.22. We did not have that much money, so I had Ruthie check the bill and we found several errors which brought it down to $26.32. Unfortunately, we did not have that much either. So we prayed. I was impressed to look in my purse and get all the change in the car. We did and it was the exact amount to the penny! Now what?

It was Sunday morning and we had no money, food, or lodging but we had God's Word that He would never fail us and He had never yet. So we prayed. Then the Father said, "Go to the church." So we packed up the car and drove back into the town and asked the Lords' help in knowing which church to attend.

On our way we passed a Western Sizzlin Steak House. I said we were eating lunch there. They all agreed that would be nice. Then suddenly I said, "Russell, turn here," and we did. There was a large Assembly of God Church. When we went in, the Pastor noticed the cross and asked Russell to go up and say a few words. When Russell saw the large crowd of people, he said, "My, there's so many of you." They all laughed, then he simply shared Jesus. It was so anointed. After church, a family asked if they could take us out for dinner. Guess where? The Western Sizzlin we had passed! Another lady handed me a check and said God told her we needed that $100 more than Sears. Others blessed us with smaller amounts of money. Praise God, everything was taken care of: gas for the car, money for food and lodging.

One of my greatest desires was to meet Arthur Blessitt. I had carried his book, *ARTHUR THE PILGRIM,* along with me every day we walked the cross. One day, we had walked many up and down hills and were very tired. We had been watching the time, anxiously awaiting the time for Ruthie to pick us up. At 5:30, there was no sign of Ruthie. At 6:00 still no Ruthie. It was beginning to get dark, so we sat along the side of the road. It was now 6:30 and still no Ruthie. We were beginning to get a little worried.

She finally drove up as though nothing was wrong. She was so excited saying, "You won't believe where we're spending the night. At the same farm Arthur Blessitt stayed when he walked the cross through here." I got so excited to think I was going to be sleeping in the same bed Arthur slept in years ago. Nancy, our host, was very nice and showed us pictures of her and Arthur when he was there. It was a special time for me.

We had walked to Mt. Vernon and the traffic was very heavy. There was little ministry but a lot of reaction to the cross. As we walked by the airport, the traffic was backed up for miles. So thousands and thousands of people, seeing the cross, had to make some kind of decision about Jesus. I was so surprised at the reaction of the people, hearing the horrible things that men in suits and who drove the expensive cars would say. Many of these were probably governmental officials yelling out these awful things at us. It was the only place in America that we have walked where we were so persecuted. We just kept smiling and saying, "Jesus loves you. Give your life to Jesus. He has a wonderful plan for your life. He will bring peace and joy to your life."

A few people gave us thumbs up. But for the most part, most people were very negative. It was such a surprise for us considering all the hundreds of people who came to the cross all through the walk.

We Made It!

Our last day of the walk took us into Washington. The morning hours took us along the Potomac River. It was so beautiful with the nicely landscaped river on one side and the huge mansions on the other. After walking for what seemed to be hours, we could find no public restroom and I had to go. So at one point I told Russell to stop. He said, "Not here!" I said, "Yep!" I took off my wagon and my orange jacket and walked under this beautiful tree that had its branches going down to the ground. I guess I just thought with Russell standing up by the road you couldn't see what I was doing under that tree even though you could see through the branches. When I went back to prepare to walk Russell said, "I can't believe this is the same lady who I began this walk with. The one who said, 'No woods for me.'" It's funny how we change our lives and ways of thinking. Self no longer matters, only Jesus.

At one point along the park area of the Potomac we had a policeman stop us and tell us we had to get off the road. Again, as I had so many other times I used the story about the news covering our story and reminded him that with our orange jackets we had a legal right to walk on any secondary highway in America. He finally said we were right in what we said and were doing. The police department was told by a very high ranking official to get us off the road no matter what it took to do so. He said, "Go on, you have a higher authority than this government official walking with you." Praise God for His wisdom and favor!

When we walked over I-95 with its many lanes of traffic we would stand and hold the cross up right and wave at the cars below. Many truck drivers honked but it would anger many of the "suits" (business men in nice cars).

We loved it however. As we walked through Alexandria several pastors, at different times, came out and walked with us. It was a great encouragement. However, as we crossed the bridge over the Potomac into Washington, this time there was no fanfare and no news coverage, only two cross carriers along with lots of cars and lots of people. Yet, as my feet hit that bridge a joy sprang up in my heart. I could hardly contain it. We did it! We had carried the cross for 900 plus miles for Jesus. Doing what he had instructed us to do. We hadn't quit or given up through all the hard times. He saw us through. Thank you, Jesus!

We passed out thousands of tracts. And as we walked the steps of the Lincoln Memorial we were both so full of joy at what the Lord had done through two ordinary people, whose lives had been broken, and in the world's eyes, were failures. But God took those pieces of broken clay and molded them into vessels He could use for His service. Praise the Lord!

Crosswalk Ministries

It was while we were sitting on the steps of the Lincoln Memorial that Russell looked up and saw a street sign. He said, "Dorothy, look at that sign." It said "Crosswalk." It was a sign telling people where they could cross the street. "Yes," I shouted, "That's it! We shall call the name of the ministry Crosswalk Ministries." For weeks we had tried to think of a name and one day I said, "God will give us the name when we get to Washington." There it was! Thank you, Jesus!

When we arrived back in Ocala after our 60 days of being on the road, few people had any interest at all in what God had done. We were so happy and full we wanted to share it with everyone but there were few listeners. The Pastor of the church we were attending allowed us to share our story in a Tuesday night service and only a hand full of people showed up. Neither the Pastor nor any of the board members or ministry teams thought it was important enough to show up. After all God had done!

We had ministered in so many churches, schools and colleges, challenging them to be bold for Jesus; yet our own church wasn't interested. It broke my heart. Then Jesus showed me how in His own home town He could do no mighty works. He said, "Just keep your eyes focused on Me."

The weeks and months that followed were very hard. It seemed as though the ministry had stopped. Russell and Ruthie both went to work in a kid's camp and I stayed home. With bills mounting and the financial pressure so great, I would take things out of the storage units and have yard sales only to lose thousands of dollars because of the rains that would come.

"Father, why?" I would cry. "You must help me." Then I began taking things from my home and going to the flea market and selling them. All I could think of was being free from the financial pressures and going out and sharing Jesus. I had a crystal bell collection that I had been collecting for many years; the bells were my prize possession. I said, "Lord, You have required so much," but I took them and began to sell them at a fraction of what they were worth. Then it was like the Lord said, "It's enough!"

Breakthrough

One day while I was driving to Orlando the Lord spoke to my heart and said, "Give TV-55 one hundred prints of the Bride for their telethon." I argued with the Lord and said, "I've tried to have Claud Bowers, the owner of TV-55, tell the story of the painting twice before and he just simply was not interested; what should change now?" And God said, "Just do as I say, I will move on him by My Spirit." With that reassurance I drove over to the TV station.

The telethon at that time was not doing so well and when I told Claud what the Spirit of God told me he said he'd try them. It was all by the move of the Holy Spirit. All Claud did was hold up the painting and briefly spoke about it and within a few hours all of them were gone. When I arrived home later that evening he called and asked if he could have more. The next afternoon he did a phone interview with me for the telethon then asked if I could come down for that evening and be on the air with him talking about the painting. Excited, I knew this was a real move of the Holy Spirit. My friend Charlotte and I went to the station for the evening telethon. Whenever I spoke on the painting telling the story and message of The Bride, the phones wouldn't stop ringing and on it went night after night. By the time it was over thousands of prints were given away.

One blind man who had been listening to the TV in his home asked the Lord, "Please open my eyes so I can see this painting," and his eyes were immediately opened. Praise the Lord! There were so many stories of healings, salvation and special moves of the Holy Spirit from us telling the story of the painting on TV that the news quickly spread to other Christian TV stations.

Camp was over for Russell and he had no place to go so I said he could stay with us. He got a job and was able to help bring funds into the home. As the fall months went on I noticed him getting weaker and weaker, something was wrong. One day he just laid on the couch and we knew he had to go to the hospital. Again he received the report that he was a juvenile diabetic. We knew he was healed. I saw it and Russell felt it. It had to be another attack of Satan to stop Russell from going on the walks we were planning. He said, "This isn't going to stop us. Crosswalk Ministries was ordained by God and we're not quitting."

Don't Quit

This is the message that comes to us time and time again. Many times you feel like you just can't make it another day. Tough times come and you think they are going to overtake you. DON'T QUIT. If it's standing for a healing, finances, a different job, doing what you feel God had told you to do, or whatever, DON'T QUIT standing.

Remember, you are more than a conqueror through Him Who loves you (Romans 8:37). Also, you can do all things through Christ Who gives you strength (Philippians 4:13). These words found in James 1:2–7 will encourage you.

My brethren, count it all joy when ye fall into divers temptations;

Knowing this, that the trying of your faith worketh patience.

But let patience have her perfect work, that ye may be perfect and entire, wanting nothing.

If any of you lack wisdom, let him ask of God, that giveth to all men liberally, and upbraideth not; and it shall be given him.

But let him ask in faith, nothing wavering. For he that wavereth is like a wave of the sea driven with the wind and tossed. For let not that man think that he shall receive anything of the Lord.

Second Corinthians 5:7 says, *"For we walk by faith, not by sight."* Don't look at the circumstances or trials that surround you, but rather stand on the Word and what it has to say about your situation.

For example, for your healing, the Word says, *"By his stripes you were healed"* (1 Peter 2:24). Believe it and stand on that promise. For your finances there are so many verses, but one of my favorites is, *"My God shall supply all my needs according to His riches in glory by Christ Jesus"* (Philippians 4:19). DON'T QUIT believing!

Put into action the words of Jesus, in Mark 11:22–24.

And Jesus answering saith unto them, Have faith in God.

For verily I say unto you, That whosoever shall say unto this mountain, Be thou removed, and be thou cast into the sea; and shall not doubt in his heart, but shall believe that those things which he saith shall come to pass; he shall have whatsoever he saith.

Therefore I say unto you, Whatsoever things ye desire, when ye pray, believe that ye receive them, and ye shall have them.

Speak to the mountain in your life, and if you believe in your heart and doubt not, you shall have whatever you say. Speak life and not death to your situation. Don't change your confession. Just simply believe God's promises and DON'T QUIT!!!

To God Be the Glory for
the Great Things He Has Done!

We prayed, "Father we are willing vessels to be used for Your service. You fill our schedule with where You want us to go."

When you commit your ways to God, He will open the doors He wants you to walk through. The Word says, *"The steps of a good man are ordered of the Lord"* (Psalm 37:23). So we simply stood on that verse. Wow, what a year we had!

We were invited to go to numerous Christian TV stations with The Bride print. So we'd minister on TV in the evening and walk the cross during the day. Owner of Dove Broadcasting, liked our ministry and sent us from one of his stations to another. In those early years he would pay our gas to get there and give us a place to stay. Our food and living we had to stand in faith for. Often times we had no money for food and we would eat whatever food was brought into the TV stations, sometimes it was just desserts.

I'll never forget when we were at the station in Myrtle Beach and we had been living on a lot of popcorn. It was a Friday night and after

Niteline, which was their live nightly program, a lady handed me $20. To us at that time it was like $100. I thought, *Great! Tonight we can eat.*

Then the Lord spoke to my heart and said, "See that lady over there? Give it to her, she has a special need." So I went to her and said, "The Lord told me to give this to you as you have a special need." She began to weep. She was in desperate need of that money and had to have it that night. Praise the Lord! It blessed me so to give it to her.

Then I went to Russell and said, "The Lord blessed us, He gave us $20." Russell said, "Cool! Wow! We can go eat." I said, "Well, ah, I gave it away." "You did what?" he said. Then I proceeded to tell him what happened and he quickly agreed it was the Lord.

That night someone took us out to eat. The next day we were working around the station and another lady came by and said the Lord spoke to her and told her to give us $100. Praise the Lord!

You must learn to be sensitive to the voice of the Lord or you could really miss a great blessing.

One night we were on TV in Monroe, Louisiana, and again, we were without funds and I had runs in my nylons. I said, "Lord, You're my provider and as a minster of the Gospel to go on the air with runs is not a good witness. I need nylons." Before the program went on the air, a lady come to me and said, "The Lord spoke to me today at work and told me you needed nylons, so I brought you five pairs." God your Father cares about your every need!

He also cares about your desires. We were in Portland, Oregon and a church took us to the Passion play. At this time Russell and I had only $2 to our name. Everyone was getting buckets of popcorn and drinks to take into the amphitheater. We stood there and said, "If we spend this last $2 on popcorn we will need something to drink and there's not enough money for both." All of a sudden two strangers walked up and said, "Would you like this bucket of popcorn? We got two and we will never be able to eat both of them." Then some friends from the church came up and got us drinks.

One time, after we had finished ministering in Louisville, Kentucky, we had only enough money to get back to Florida. My parents lived in Shipshewana, Indiana and I really wanted to see them, so we prayed and headed for their house. We knew there wasn't enough money to go there and then back to Florida. The past week in Louisville had been one with many long hours. I fell asleep as Russell was driving. After some time I woke up just in time to see a rest area ahead. I asked Russell to please stop.

While I went to the restroom a lady, seeing Crosswalk Ministries and the large cross on the side of our van, came over and asked Russell if he was a minister. She proceeded to tell him that her mother was dying and she needed prayer. As I came back towards the van I saw Russell standing in front of the van praying with her. I felt led to give her a Bride print. Meanwhile, another minister stopped and prayed also. When he saw the picture he said he wanted to buy some. He bought $200 worth. Not only did a lady get ministered to, we also received the extra money we needed.

What an awesome Father we have!

Old pictures clipped from a
newspaper back in the day

Freak snow storm in New Mexico

Russell walking through New York City—Larry King in the background

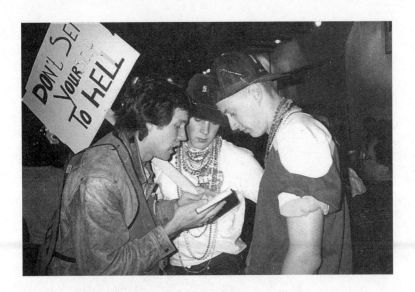

Russell witnessing at Mardi Gras in New Orleans

Me, witnessing on the streets of Portland, Oregon

Russell ministering to a young boy in Chicago, Illinois

Russell, Randy, and me

Russell and me with Arthur and Denise Blessitt in
Tampa, Florida

Arthur, Denise, me, and Russell

Our homeless camp in Portland, Oregon

Just the two of us, walking a bridge in Portland, Oregon

Carrying the cross daily

Passing through Chimayo, New Mexico

Me and Russell in Monroe, Louisiana

Me, holding the cross in Portland, Maine

Experiencing the Myrtle Beach Parade

Hosting KMCT TV-39

Uncle Russ & Kids Company, KMCT TV-39

The Santa Fe Miracle

We were on our way to Santa Fe, New Mexico to help a TV station. That morning before we left, Charles Reed, the manager of the Monroe, Louisiana station said, "You two are braver than I am taking that old car across the desert, you will be lucky to make it to the Texas border." We sort of smiled and said, "God takes care of us."

Before we ever got to the Texas border we had to pull the car over as it was over heating. We laid hands on the car and committed it to Him, filled it with water and on we went, driving day and night to get there. We were in the desert on Highway 40 in New Mexico about 60 miles from Santa Fe. It was my shift to drive and Russell was sound asleep.

All of a sudden the car began to lose power. Then it started clanging and making a loud noise. This woke Russell and he asked what was happening. I told him I didn't know but there was no power. I pulled the car off the side of the road, and Russell looked under the hood and said, "I think we've blown the engine." He began to get angry with God. We had just had a great revival in Louisiana where many people were ministered to and saved and here we were with a blown engine.

Now because I had been more experienced in the things of God, I said, "Russell, your being angry isn't going to solve a thing. We must praise God in every situation. He's our only help now." We had only $14 to our name. You may say, "How could you take off across the desert with an old car and only enough money to get there? Isn't that foolish?"

I would say, as my friend Arthur Blessitt says, "If God told you to go to New York and you don't have the money for the plane ticket then take the bus! If you don't have the money for a bus ticket, then drive! If you don't have the money for gas, then walk! If you can't walk, then fall in that direction! It's His problem to get you there not yours. You must be willing to be obedient."

There was a reason for this. So I just began to praise Him as Russell was slamming the car doors. Soon a trucker stopped. He came with a jug of water. Russell mumbled, "A lot of good that's going to do." I told him to be quiet and to change his attitude. The trucker confirmed we had a blown engine and said he would drive me up the road to get a wrecker. Now I just happened to have my son's AAA card with me and it was good for 10 miles towing. Would you believe it, we were eight miles from the station. Praise the Lord! So we had it towed. The trucker, before he left, said that the Lord impressed him to give me $100. I never spoke our need, he just did it.

At the station where we had the car towed, another man had just driven up with a flatbed trailer. His daughter had broken down there the week before and he came to pick up her car. He asked Russell about the cross on the top of our car and asked where we were going. Russell said, "Albuquerque." He said, "Great!" so we unloaded our car into his van and put the cross and wagon on his flatbed. We were taken to Albuquerque where the son of the TV station owner picked us up and took us on into Santa Fe. What a blessing, how God sent first the truck driver, then the man with the flatbed and then got us into Santa Fe. Russell said, "Lord I'm sorry for letting my flesh rule." Every time you go through a trial it strengthens you to walk in more trust with Jesus. This was only the beginning of our trials in New Mexico.

The next three days we were on TV. Russell drove a borrowed truck back to the station to where our car had been towed and then to a dealer's lot that was recommended to us. We found out it was too old to put a new engine into it. So God would really have to move a mountain to get us back. It was Friday night the last night of the telethon. We were handed a check for $500.

By now we had zero money and a check for $500 which we couldn't cash. It was Sunday morning, and time to check out of the motel and go where? No money and a check that couldn't be cashed! We prayed, "Lord, what shall we do?" He impressed us to call a lady we had met and ask her if we could go to church with her. She said great, I'll pick you up. She knew of our car situation and asked what we were going to do. I said we didn't know, so she said we were going to stay with her until we could work something out.

That morning after church Russell overheard someone speaking to this lady's husband. They said, "We hear you are having Russell and Dorothy stay with you. What a blessing." He said, "I'm glad you think so." Russell was crushed. Monday came and we cashed the $500 check and gave these people $300 of it for letting us stay there. Russell felt it might make the man happier that we were there.

During the day we would walk the cross around Santa Fe then, in the evening, we would get back to the house in time to cook the evening meal. Every day we were there, we bought groceries out of the $200 we had left as not to be a burden on these people.

One day as we were walking, we were stopped by three men from "Burros for Jesus" in Albuquerque, New Mexico. Daw Sanchez, the pastor and founder of "Burros for Jesus," loved what we were doing and asked us to come down and minister to their people. Their ministry is a halfway house for those leaving prison and preparing to go back into society. I believe it is a six month program. Also, it's a place that people go to, who are coming off drugs. We said we would love to come, but couldn't, as we had no vehicle to get there. We told them what had happened to our car. Then they came into agreement in prayer that God would provide us with another car. Their short visit with us was a time of real encouragement.

Day after day went by with the man asking us what we were doing about getting a car or how we were planning to leave there. We kept telling him God was working something out on our behalf. Daily, with that unwanted pressure, I would say, "Jesus help us, we've got to get out of here."

Soon, almost a week had passed and it was Good Friday. We heard of the walk to Chimayo, was a walk made by hundreds of people. Some walked hundreds of miles, doing penance for their sins. Some would beat themselves with whips. Others would put thorns on their heads, or exact against themselves whatever penance they felt they had to do. So Russell and I were excited to make this walk. We were able to lead numbers of people to Jesus, telling them the price for all their sins had already been paid for by the shed blood of Jesus. Nothing you do will bring you salvation. Only by accepting Jesus as your Lord and Savior can you have forgiveness of your sins.

It was an awesome time! The next week we ran into the owner of the TV station. He asked what we were still doing there. I told him we were stuck until the Lord worked something out for us. He said, "Well, since you're still here, why don't you come down and be on the air with me?" I said okay. He had a morning program so, after the program, we'd go out into the streets with the cross.

We had been staying with these people for nearly a week and a half now and the pressure was getting stronger from the man for us to get out. We both felt so helpless. One afternoon while we walked the cross to the town square, I just couldn't witness sitting on a park bench. The tears began to pour down my face and I reached into my purse for a

Kleenex and pulled out my business Bible along with the Kleenex. I wiped the tears from my eyes and opened the Bible and began to read from *The Bible Incorporated.*

> Lift up your eyes to the hills from where your help comes, the Lord, who made heaven and earth. Be glad and rejoice in His mercy: for He has considered your trouble, and knows the anguish of your soul. He has not given you into the enemy's hands: He has set your feet in a large place. God brings you out of the horrible pit and the miry clay to set your feet upon a rock, and establish your goings.
>
> Let not your heart be troubled; you believe in God, believe also in Jesus. Though you walk in the midst of trouble, He will revive you and perfect that which concerns you. For the Lord is good, a stronghold in the day of trouble; and He knows them that trust in Him, and has promised to supply all your need according to His riches in glory by Christ Jesus.

I repented for being so weary and not praising the Lord in this situation. New strength came. All of a sudden the square was full of children and young people, punk rockers, and New Age believers. We began to walk the cross around the square. Many mocked and jeered, others yelled out hateful things. Many grown people hate the name of Jesus. One man gave Russell such a hard time about the wheel on the cross, Russell answered, "Jesus loves you."

It seemed as if we were the only believers on the square. Soon Russell was surrounded with 15 or 20 young boys. They began to laugh and poke fun at Russell; I stayed back and prayed. Russell opened his mouth with such anointing, asking them if they believed in God. They laughed and said, "We are god, the trees are god, the grass is god." Such New Age thinking and beliefs had already been instilled in these young minds.

Then Russell began to tell the simple Good News Gospel. When he had finished, he said, "Is there anyone who believes what I've told you, and who would be man enough to come up here and put your hands on this cross and ask Jesus into your heart?" One little boy came forward with tears in his eyes and said, "Mister, I believe what you're saying is true and I want Jesus to come into my life." The other boys began to laugh and to make fun of him saying, "Don't do it." He ignored them and repeated the Sinners Prayer while his friends were laughing at him in the background. It was like God had put a shield around him. When he was finished repeating the prayer with Russell, his face shined with the glory of God. I shall never forget it. He turned to his friends and said, "This is real!" Praise the Lord!

It was a hot day and Russell said, "I wish we could just have a snow storm," and I said, "So why don't you pray for it?" So he did. By 4:30 that afternoon the temperature had dropped and by 8:00 the ground was covered with snow and we were throwing snowballs. The news said we had a freak snow storm but we knew it was to bless Russell.

That night I thanked the Father for the miracles of the day and said, "Father, what's really happening here?" He led me to the story of the Good Samaritan found in Luke 10:25–37. I asked Him who that related to. He said we were as the man lying on the side of the road and there was a man (whom He named to me) that He wanted to bless but He wanted to give him an opportunity to be a blessing.

The man had known the need and was passing by on the other side. The confirmation of what the Lord had said came to me later when I was told this man had a new vehicle that was sitting outside of his building that hadn't been used in close to a year. He was a very wealthy man whom the Father wanted to bless in a special way. He saw our need but never reached out to help. The Lord assured me not to worry; when one person isn't obedient, He was still Lord and we would be leaving soon.

We were invited to visit with a lady named Rainbow. She is a great artist. What a neat and wonderful lady she was! As we ate she told us she was in hiding from people who wanted to drag her back into the occult.

According to her, years ago, she was the one who taught Prince how to use color with music, to program what they wanted into people's minds.

Before we left she handed me some jewelry her father, who was a very famous craftsman, had made and she said that it would buy us a vehicle. These pieces were very precious to her because they were left to her by her father. We had the jewelry appraised and it was valued at $3,800. However, while in Santa Fe, we couldn't find anyone who would trade a vehicle for the jewelry.

We had just finished the program and Russell and I were standing there saying, "Oh Lord, now what?" The phone rang and it was for us. My heart began pounding as I heard the caller say, "If you can get down here to Albuquerque, we have a vehicle that will be ready for you sometime this afternoon." "Burros for Jesus," the ministry we had talked to the week before, took an old car and fixed it up for us.

The Lord, again, reminded me of the Good Samaritan story, how He gave the chance to someone who could well afford to help us, and had a vehicle in hand to help us, but he passed by on the other side. Instead, here came a man along who had little and gave much; it was a great example to me.

Now we had to get from Santa Fe to Albuquerque. Again Russell and I prayed. So we decided to see what a rental car would cost us. When we opened the phone book we found there were numerous rental car places. Russell pointed to one called "The Ugly Duckling" and said to call that one. The owner answered and when he heard who I was, he said that our old car was parked on his repair lot. He felt in his heart that he was to help us in some way. So he said he would come over to the TV station and pick us up and we could borrow his truck, pick up the car and bring it back the next day with no charge to us. We just couldn't stop praising the Lord for all he had done.

It was Sunday afternoon and we were heading back to Monroe, Louisiana with the 1976 Mercury car this wonderful ministry had blessed us with. We were just praising the Lord for His handiwork. Again driving through the night, when it was my shift to drive, I found it very hard to shift gears. It got so hard Russell had to take over and drive the rest of the way into Monroe. At the last stop sign before we got to the TV station in Monroe, the car would no longer shift and we coasted into the TV station parking lot.

The mechanic that worked around there checked the car out for us and asked us, "How did you get this car here?" We said we drove it. He said, "Impossible, there are no bolts holding up the transmission." Thank you Jesus for Your angels who held the transmission in place long enough to get us there.

The manager of the TV station is Charles Reed, who over the years has proven to be a great friend to this ministry. If we were stranded anywhere he would be there for us and we love him for that. He is a true friend!

Anyway, we helped him at the station for the next several weeks. He told us he was going to see to it that we would get another car, one we could count on. I told Russell we had prayed for a van and God was going to give us a van. Every time Charles said something about the car I smiled and said to myself, "Thank you, Lord, for our van."

That week we walked the cross around the area of the TV station and through some of Monroe. We were on the corner of a four lane highway, waiting at a traffic light, when a man in a pickup truck pulled over on a side street. He slammed the door of his truck and began heading our way. He was a real hard-core redneck. The closer he came he dropped to his knees and began crawling to the cross. He grabbed a hold of the cross and hung on for dear life. Sobbing and sobbing, he said, "I need Jesus, help me Jesus."

The power of the cross going down the road is awesome. We also walked the cross through the school playgrounds. Kids surrounded us and wanted to know what we were doing. We shared in a simple way about Jesus. You must be real with children, show them love and they will receive what you have to tell them. They all said the salvation prayer.

Several asked us to pray for other things such as, "Lord, help me to quit smoking." One wanted us to pray for his mother and father to quit fighting. These children were like sponges, soaking up all we were telling them.

Just after we had led these children to Jesus, the devil sent a man over and he told the children not to listen to us. "Jesus is dead," he said, "The Holy Spirit is hoodoo."

Russell began speaking to the man but he wouldn't listen or be quiet, he just got louder. Now the Word says the demons tremble at the name of Jesus so I just went to him and said with great authority, "In the name of Jesus, I command your mouth to be shut and you must leave this place now." With that the man quietly turned around and walked away. The Bible says we have authority in the name of Jesus so learn to use it! Don't get into fear in a bad situation. Know who you are in Christ Jesus and in His name move out with authority!

We walked in one area and a Vietnam veteran came to the cross. He was hard and very arrogant. We just talked with him a while, then asked him if Russell could pray with him. While Russell prayed, I put my arm around him and place my hand on his chest. Russell placed his hand on the man's shoulder, and as Russell began praying the power of God fell on the man and he began crying. He said, "Why are you making me cry?" We told him it was Jesus.

He said he had not cried since Vietnam. He said he had to kill all those children and people and it made him very hard to live with. When his mother and grandmother died he wanted to cry but couldn't, and we were making him cry. With that I hugged him and just stood there holding him as his tears soaked my blouse. Russell was able to lead him to Jesus. He followed us everywhere we went and told everyone he came in contact with, "Listen to what they have to say. It's real. I feel so clean and new, you need Jesus. Listen to them."

The power of God is seen. You will never experience this power just going to church weekly and getting fat on the Word. You must give out to others. See them through the eyes of Jesus. *Get a burden for the lost and hurting in this world.*

Here it was Saturday night and we were to leave Monday and there still wasn't a vehicle because a man said he could fix our car but he hadn't done it yet. It was Sunday morning and we were in church when Pastor Charles Reed told the story of our need for a vehicle to the people. He said, "I have a hundred dollars for another car for Russell and Dorothy. Who will help me?"

I felt like crawling under the seat. I just wasn't used to getting offerings. Before it was over they had collected around $900 from that small congregation. Ted Barns, another great friend, said he knew of a place where he could get us a car at a good price. So they gave him the money. When we were alone I said, "Russell, by tonight we will have us a van." As we drove into church that night I saw a yellow van parked right in front of the church. I said, "That's our van."

Sure enough, Ted met us at the door and handed Russell the keys. He said, "Drive it and see if you like it." We were so excited because God has given us a van just as He promised. Ted said that when the man he purchased the van from heard what is was for he sold it to him for $700 leaving us $200 for gas to get home! Hallelujah! We gave the car to a street evangelist. He said he could have it fixed; he had been believing for a car so it was a blessing to him. How exciting it is to see God working in our lives on our behalf. If you keep standing, there's always victory! In my diary at this point I wrote, "God is not finished yet. I see a silver and burgundy van coming to us. Yes, I receive it!"

Myrtle Beach

After Louisiana, we were asked to help the television station in Myrtle Beach. What a neat place to witness for Jesus. We would be on TV at night and walk the cross during the day. You should have seen all the shocked looks the day we walked the cross down the beach. People couldn't believe their eyes. What a great fish hook the cross is—a lot of people came to the cross just out of curiosity, while others came because they truly needed a life change in their hearts.

One day, while walking on a long stretch up the coast, there was a man on a motorcycle who stopped us and asked if we knew where they were going to have the human sacrifice that night. We tried to witness Jesus to him but he was a Satanist and would not hear. Then within minutes several cars went by and yelled out, "Satan rules!" As you walk through areas you can feel the demonic forces. We began to do spiritual warfare, taking dominion over the ground we were on and as far as we could see. We prayed that the principalities that ruled that area would lose their hold and the righteous would rule. About one area the police said, "Don't go in there, they will kill you." Knowing we had authority through Jesus, we went in. They were doing drugs everywhere; the cross made quite a stir. A man came up to me and said, "Don't you know you're in the devil's territory? You've got to get out of here." I said, "No sir, you're wrong! The Word of God says everywhere I put my feet He has given it to me, and in the name of Jesus, I claim this land for Jesus. You will either have to give your life to Jesus or leave this place." He just shook his head and left.

We talked to another young man. You could see how he had lived a very rough life. His shirt was off and you could see all the scars from when he was shot and knifed. One of his ears was partially cut off and his throat had been sliced. Tears came to my eyes as he said, "God? There is no God." We asked him why he would feel that way. It seems as a young child his parents had left him there to fend for himself. I asked him if I could hug him and he just looked at me strangely. When I hugged him the power of God went through him and he began to cry like a baby. Russell talked to him about Jesus and led him to the Lord.

Don't ever, when you're witnessing, be afraid to put your arms around a dirty person. Let the compassion of Jesus go through you and minister to that person. Many people haven't been hugged in years. When we left that area we found a group of on-fire Christians who said they would keep on ministering there and work with this young man. Myrtle Beach, like so many other beaches, attracts the young people. You will find many runaways along with high school and college kids out there drinking, drugging, and having sex. What an area to share Jesus. They are all searching for a good thing but when the party is over, then what? The scars can go on for a lifetime unless someone reaches out in love, not condemnation, and shares Jesus with them.

Greetings From Salem, Oregon and— Our Wedding!

June and July in Oregon are breathtakingly beautiful. Roses and flowers bloom everywhere you look, and the mountains are so majestic. It took us four days to drive there, driving around the clock. We thank God for our van which was given to us, as it made our trips so much more comfortable. I drove during the day while Russell slept and he drove during the night while I slept. We took the Northern route coming here, and all I could do was thank the Father day by day and mile by mile that He gave me eyes to see all the beauty of His handiwork.

Oregon is such a mission field. They say that less than 2 percent of the people go to church here. Portland has over 1,000 kids on the street at any one time. There is even a bridge called "suicide bridge" and the suicide rate is one of the highest in the nation. Prostitution here starts at 12 years of age, both male and female. Portland is ranked fifth in the nation for major crimes, murder, rape, robbery and burglary. Drugs give it one of the highest overdose rates in the nation. Alcohol, cults, Satanism, gang violence, and demon possession run rampant. The population rose 29 percent, crime rose 84 percent, and violent crime rose 175 percent. Portland has the highest per capita homosexual population in the nation. There are great churches here, plus Teen Challenge, YWAM, and others who are reaching out in these areas and making a difference.

Russell and I were blessed when we carried the cross and passed out hundreds of tracts at the Portland Rose Festival along with Teen Challenge and YWAM. People's lives were changed and much good seed was planted.

Another way of making a difference is through Christian television. Dove Broadcasting paid our gas to the neighboring city of Salem.

We volunteered our time, and worked at the station every day and night. I was the producer of all the live programs we aired every night and Russell worked around the station, doing whatever he was needed to do. He also ran camera, did floor directing, and was my right hand man in production. We also hosted a four hour live program together every night, seven nights a week. It was very taxing, with little sleep and much hard work. But the rewards were great when people called in and were saved.

With Salem being the capital city of Oregon, Christian television can help make the difference in the political arena, as we exposed on the air daily what the devil was doing through politics. We had a strong Christian lobbyist who came on the air and told the truth about what was happening. Christians cannot get the complete news just from secular stations. We can band together and make a difference.

Carl Becker, a pastor full of zeal for the Lord, with members of his church, along with others who love Jesus, walked the cross with Russell and me every Sunday afternoon, praying for the leaders of the state. We prayed that they would become men and women of God, and for revival to come to the northwest. We were able to help him with this great endeavor by airing it on TV and, as a result, many other pastors and prayer warriors joined him.

Russell and I have walked the cross through the streets of Salem, Portland, and in the Strawberry Festival Parade in Lebanon with Teen

Challenge. There were more than 25,000 people in attendance and we have seen people's lives changed, healings, and more. God is so good!

Many times I would ask the Father, "What are we doing in Oregon when I should be out walking with the cross? Are we really making a difference?" He then showed me the thousands of people whose lives we touched on the air every night and so gently said to me, "You are right where I want you to be." I said, "Thank you, Father for choosing us to be used of You in this way."

We were there five months on this trip. The Lord met our needs daily down to the smallest detail. We never asked for anything, and yet He supplied our every need. There were many days when we were down to pocket change and someone would say, "Here's some gas money," or, "The Lord told me to give you these groceries." Or they would hand Russell some ties for him and nylons for me or money for a new dress, or even take me downtown and buy me new shoes the very day mine wore out.

What a mighty good God we serve! We have learned how to enter into His rest knowing He supplies everything we have need of. He wants to do the same for you. Enter into that new realm with Him and learn to trust Him in every area of your life. It is the greatest walk I have ever done. Try it. You will like it.

Special Note: in all these years of trusting Jesus, I truly believe one of the key reasons we were always blessed is because we always gave tithes and offerings on every dollar we received. Tithing shows evidence in where you put your trust. If you are not blessed, check out your tithes and offerings record. The Lord wants you to be blessed, so that you can be a blessing to help spread the Gospel.

Those five months spent in Oregon were some of the greatest times I have ever had. We both loved it so much. The people became like my family. My daughter was having some hard times back in Florida and I missed her so much. I prayed and asked the Father to please give me the money to bring her out there to stay with us. Within a few days I was given enough money for a bus ticket for her to come. I could hardly wait for her to get there.

Russell had been talking to Pastor Becker about going to RHEMA Bible Training Center. It was always his desire to go to school. At this time I thought it would be a good change for both of us, as we had not been separated other than his time at summer camp. When I prayed about it, God clearly spoke to me and said to let him go. At first I was very happy for him to go. But as the day for him to leave grew closer, I began to cry a lot. I did not understand what was happening. He was just like one of my kids, I thought, and when the other children left for school or whatever, I was very happy for them.

We had planned one last cross walk from Portland to Salem. This was a 73-mile walk and would take us three days. We invited the friends of the station to walk with us. It was a wonderful time as we had a lot of people to make this walk on and off. One little boy named Joshua, probably about nine years old or so, walked with us. He was so neat. He said, "I'd do anything for Jesus. I'd even throw myself into that there sticker bush for Him." With all those people it made a great statement. Again, the cross got a lot of news coverage.

The day came to drive Russell to the airport in Portland. I fought to keep the tears back. I guess I thought it would be the end of Crosswalk Ministries. Tammy was a great comfort during this time. We grew so close as she became the station receptionist and my right hand. Daily I would see her grow in the Word. What a blessing she was!

There was a pastor who wanted to ordain me. I was very happy because this was a desire of my heart, to forever preach the Gospel. I will never as long as I live forget the feeling I had when the pastor and the elders of the church laid hands on me. The anointing was so strong. I felt it run through me. Thank You Jesus, for choosing me.

The next weeks without Russell seemed endless. I was missing him so much. Soon I began to write to him daily, then calling daily. He would tell me how great everything was and how he was running the center TV camera on the Kenneth Hagin program. The teaching was wonderful, but then there would be a drop in his voice. "I miss you and I miss us ministering together," he would say. "I have already experienced the power of God when we minister and I'm not seeing that in the graduates here. Instead when I go to a gas station I see people who graduated three or four years ago working there and they are still waiting on the Lord. I don't want that to happen to me." As the weeks went on, I could feel more and more of Russell's discontent.

We had some very dear Jewish friends whom I would often put on the air. One night while one was there, he leaned over and said, "Dorothy, don't think it's strange what you're feeling for Russell. God uses the strange things to confound the wise. What you're feeling is of God. You should quit fighting it and give into it."

Then, that same night, a pastor's wife said, "I sure wish you would give up to what God wants you to do. He has had me up praying for you every night around 3:00 in the morning." I said, "How can this be? Russell is years younger than me and we would never be accepted in the ministry." She said, "That's not your problem. Hasn't God used you so far? What's to change?"

Russell sent me a card and said he felt we should get married and he said that when I came back through Tulsa, we would talk about it.

Owners of the Oregon station, loved my daughter, Tammy and me, and we could have stayed at the television station forever. They wanted me to run it permanently, but I had already made prior commitments for November and December and I would have to keep them. It was our last night on the air in Oregon. We had built a new studio and the station was growing so fast, with so many victories. I was shocked as the station became packed with people to say good-bye. It was wonderful! My friend, Diane, who became like a sister to me, baked a cake 4 foot squared, for me. Many tears were shed as we all hugged and said good-bye. What a blessing those past months had been in our lives.

Tammy and I drove, day and night, back through the mountains and into Tulsa, Oklahoma. Russell met us there. I saw him through different eyes.

He said, "I prayed if I couldn't get peace about staying here when you came through, I was leaving." I said, "Are you sure this is what you want?"

He said, "It was great here and I'll never put it down, but we've got to keep doing what we've been doing and when I went to check out of school it was like a joy hit me. I did a little jig and said, 'I'm free.'"

So off we went, stopping in Monroe, Louisiana, then on to Myrtle Beach, South Carolina. After some talking and meeting with a dear pastor friend of ours, we decided to get married in Myrtle Beach so no one could talk us out of it when we got back to Florida. We didn't even tell any of our family or friends, except for Tammy and those at Myrtle Beach, for fear they would talk us out of getting married.

It was just a small wedding with only a few people. No tuxedos or gowns or beautiful flowers, just a simple little wedding with a lot of meaning. After the marriage ceremony, the pastor ordained Russell and me, together, to go out and preach the Gospel. We had always flowed in the Spirit as one, but now we were truly one.

The Mardi Gras Connection

I never had a full realization of a mighty warrior dressed for battle until we joined up with 1,500 other radical Christians from all across the nation and Canada, in New Orleans at Mardi Gras.

We were truly on a battlefield.

Sin City, USA. Every form of demonic activity was found there. Open sex on the streets, nudity, homosexuality, transvestites, drunkenness and so much more ran rampant through the days of Mardi Gras. People were entertaining every form of wickedness imaginable. Russell and I have walked with a wooden cross all over this nation and yet we have never seen such evil.

In preparing to go to Mardi Gras, we decided to go with Christ in Action's director, Denny Nissley, a powerful man of God, taking cities for Jesus. It was mandatory that we fast every Tuesday for two months, then the last three days before Mardi Gras. Also, we were to pray daily warfare prayers and read and learn set scriptures, preparing our hearts for the spiritual battles ahead.

Upon arrival at the church which was to house us for the next six days, we were separated. Men slept in specific classrooms and girls in other classrooms. The schedule was so strict; you soon knew you were in a boot camp preparing for war against the devil.

Our schedule was as follows: Up at 6:00 a.m. with three sinks and some 125 people. Some people got up even earlier. Then it was breakfast at 8:00, quiet time at 9:00 (the time you personally spent on your face before the Father or in the Word, strictly enforced), warfare prayer at 10:00 and worship from 10:30 to noon. Then it was lunch and girl's shower time in the baptistery. Chapel was at 1:00 p.m. and the street ministry at 1:15 until 5:00. At 5:30, it was time for supper and men's shower time. Then came chapel again at 6:30 p.m. and street ministry at 6:45, sometimes until 2:00 a.m. You were never to be late or you would miss out.

The reason I shared this with you, first, was to show that we need to have a more disciplined lifestyle in order to become more effective for the kingdom of heaven. Second, to show if you are going to go into the battlefield, you must first prepare yourself as a good soldier. Daily time in the Word, warfare prayer, praise and worship are a must before the battle.

We are fighting a spiritual battle out on the streets and you are fighting one in your daily life.

Day after day, when the Holy Ghost came upon men and women, as Denny Nissley called them to go out into the streets, you would see the power of God on street corners and throughout the streets in the French Quarter. In the midst of the foulest sins men can conjure up, there are people of all walks of life and every age, coming to the knowledge of Jesus Christ: demons being cast out, people being healed and filled with the Holy Ghost. Signs and wonders followed everywhere.

On Monday night, we came together with the other Christians at Jackson Square, who led us in praise and worship. As we were praising God with the cross standing upright before us, many banners and signs towered high above us. The Satanists and witches were doing their chants and trying to put curses on us. It was almost like in the days of Baal. The devil's priests against God's priests. We all knelt on the streets and prayed out to God in warfare prayer and shouts of victory.

Then, quickly, the Christ in Action's leaders would line us up four-abreast, locking arms with those beside us and holding to those in front of us. The crosses we placed on the outsides, banners, signs and one-half mile hailers mingled throughout the 1,500-people parade. They had runners going up and down the sides to make sure we did not break rank and to give us constant instructions.

Denny Nissley, and several other huge men, along with a large cross: 1 foot thick, 12 feet long, and 6 feet wide, led the way; following them was a battalion of strong men four abreast. The people on Bourbon Street were packed in like sardines, shoulder to shoulder, so it was most important for these "heavy weights" to separate the sea of people so we could get through. As we wound in and out of the streets heading to Bourbon Street, we sang, "Oh the Blood of Jesus." It was so power-ful. You felt as though you were in a mighty army preparing for battle. When we hit Bourbon Street, we sang it with everything that was in us. It brought a calmness as people stood back in shock and amazement to see so many Christians standing for what they believed. To some it brought so much conviction that they ran, while others fell to their knees and wanted Jesus.

When we reached Bourbon and St. Anne streets, in the homosexual section, we spread out and covered the whole street for blocks. We all fell to our knees and prayed for the city, the people, and the homo-sexuals to find Jesus. When we first fell to our knees we were told to be silent in prayer. Then we broke out with warfare prayers and praise. Standing up, we sang "All Hail the Power of Jesus Name." I wish every believer could have experienced this because it would eternally change their lives. After this, we quickly lined up, four abreast, singing praises to God and marched back to Jackson Square where we ended with a victory celebration.

When it was all over, we each went out in pairs to reap the harvest. The Satanists and witches were prayed with and MANY received Jesus and were baptized in the Holy Spirit. There were those who mocked us and carried crosses with "Pizza Saves" on them. I know of a college student who was so appalled by it that he gave his life to Jesus.

Fellow Christians, rise up! It is time to take seriously the things of the Lord. Let it not be said of us, "The harvest is ended and we are not yet saved." This is the decade of harvest. Rise up, mighty men and women of God! Prepare yourself for the daily battles ahead. Spend time daily in prayer, fasting, reading the Word, communicating with the Father and praising Him. Battles are won by praise to the Lord.

Chicago

After Mardi Gras we drove straight through to Chicago. Russell was driving while Wendy and Karen, the two girls who went with us to Mardi Gras, and I were sleeping. I awoke and looked at Russell and big old tears were just racing down his face. I said, "What's wrong, baby?" He said, "I was just talking to the Lord and telling Him there were so many fish out there who need Jesus and He said to me 'Yes, and I've given you a big pole,'" referring to the cross Russell carried.

As we drove along the streets in Chicago by Caprenio Green, the van suddenly began to smell hot and then we saw flames under the dash. Some of the wiring had caught on fire. We jumped out of the van as Russell quickly put the fire out. Karen then said, "Do you know how dangerous this area is? People shoot out of the windows at people and cars!" "Not at us," I replied, "He gives His angels charge over us." We had brought Karen up with us to work with the Caprenio Green Ministry.

It was here in Caprenio Green, during the times when things were so bad with the drug lords and gangs, that this precious little red haired pastor decided to do something to change the area.

For weeks he would go and sit on the park bench in front of the main two apartment buildings where there was continuous gun fire. While he would be sitting there, he would pass out candy bars to the children and would tell them about Jesus. In time, he was able to get a small building across from those two apartment buildings. He was able to bring the children and teach them the Word.

Soon the children of the drug lords and gang leaders, who range in ages from two to 16, were coming to this church. Quickly they were raised up in the things of the Lord. With this rapid growth, Pastor Dan saw the need for help to get into these apartment buildings and lead the families to Jesus. He could think of no better way than to train up his own army of little soldiers for Jesus.

So he developed a Bible training school and, upon completion of the course these children would become the preachers, song leaders, and spiritual leaders. When they graduated, they were given their own black leather jackets that said "Love God, Hate Sin."

These little guys now had their own gang for Jesus. They were responsible to each other and for each other. If one would mess up or get out of line they were brought in for a meeting. As time went on it became the cool thing to do to become part of God's Army.

While visiting there we helped to panel the walls of the church. As you walked in the front door you could see many bullet holes in the door and in the front of the building. Yet God protects those who go in and out of there.

We went to an evening service. It was entirely conducted by these young black leather jacket leaders. The praise was great and Pastor Dan said a few words but the ministry was done by one of the young men. When he was done preaching the altar was packed with children on their knees, crying and pouring their hearts out to God.

Then the other black jacket kids would minister to them and pray with them. My heart broke; what we had witnessed was just so powerful. As you looked around the audience there were students from Moody

Bible Institute and parents of those dear children who had found Jesus as a result of their child's witness.

The Bible says, *"A little child shall lead them"* (Isaiah 11:6).

We walked the cross through the streets of Chicago. On numerous street corners you could hear the faithful street preachers ministering, and see the different Jesus signs. We passed out lots of tracts, but did not do a lot of personal ministry. Everyone seemed to be in such a hurry.

There was a little boy who gave his heart to Jesus. He was probably eight or nine years old and all alone on the streets.

Russell can really minister to the runaways and young boys in trouble, because that was what Jesus brought him out of.

God's Special Blessings: Louisville, Kentucky

Leaving Chicago we drove straight home, 24 hours, to Ocala. It was late afternoon. When we checked our phone messages there was one from Bob Rodgers in Louisville, Kentucky. He said to call ASAP. I quickly gave him a call and he said, "I need you to come help me raise money for Hannah's House, a home for unwed mothers." He went on to say that because of the nature of the subject matter the funds were coming in slowly. I said we would come.

Now, God really had to help us. We were both tired from having just driven 24 hours straight and now we had to turn around and drive back from where we just came from. Also, there was the matter of money. We came home with $3 left to our names. We went to the post office and there were checks for three "Bride" print orders which totaled $45. Then my father said he had $20 for us, so, off we went with $65. Now, it has always taken us around $120 to go north, so God was really going to have to move. We prayed over the van and asked the Father to stretch the gas. We also watched for the cheapest gas we could find. We made it the next day with $2.50 to spare. What a major blessing!

The past two weeks had been hard ministry, first at Mardi Gras, then on to Chicago. At Mardi Gras we slept on the floor of a church and showered in the baptistery. Now the Father was really blessing us. We were given a suite with a beautiful basket of flowers. We were told we could eat anything we wanted in any of the restaurants. We were treated like kings. It was one of the Father's many blessings.

We were on the air night after night ministering about the Bride of Christ and on the painting. The phones wouldn't stop ringing.

One night a little girl called in for prayer for her mother who was a prostitute. Her story broke my heart. I prayed and asked the Father to work out some way that I could meet this little girl. The next day we went down to the street programs to help feed the poor. You'll never believe who showed up—the little girl and her aunt.

They told me the whole story of the little girl's mother. A year or so ago she got in with some very bad people. They cut her up pretty badly and threw her in the river for dead. She remembered her upbringing and said, "God, if You're real, help me." With that a log came floating by and she held onto it making her way over to the shoreline. She managed to pull herself out of the water, but she was totally naked. Seeing a light up the block she staggered toward it and, when she got there, she cried out for help. She spent the next days in intensive care.

This put a scare into her for a few weeks, but it wasn't long until she was out on the streets again. At this time her family hadn't seen or heard from her in months.

We prayed with the aunt and the little girl that the angels would help them find her mother. Assured that God would help them I said, "When you find her, we will either be at the TV station or at the hotel."

The hotel had a very exclusive restaurant and we had planned to make our last night's meal special and eat there. This was our last night so we got ready for the programs early and went out for our special meal. The violinist was playing around our table; it was a very romantic time.

When I looked up, I saw the aunt we had spoken to earlier and her sister, the prostitute standing there peering in at us. We invited them to come over and sit down with us. They said they weren't dressed good enough for this type of restaurant. I said to come and sit down anyway. We asked them if they were hungry. They both said, "No," as they could see this had to be a very expensive restaurant. So we ordered for them and said, "Jesus wants to bless you."

I could see a partial smile come on that dear girl's hardened face. We spoke to her of Jesus the entire time. It was greater than any romantic dinner that I could have had when I saw the tears come to her eyes and she accepted Jesus. My oh my, how can anyone describe that scene?

We had to leave for the programs but told them to stay as long as they wanted and to meet us at the TV station.

What a great stir that caused on TV that night! I could hardly contain myself as I spoke of the goodness and mercy of our loving Father.

When it was all said and done we had raised enough money to completely finish and furnish Hannah's House.

Praise the Lord!

God Changes Our Plans: Street Reach of Portland, Oregon

We were sent an invitation to go to Russia and carry the cross. At that time there was no money to go. We were asked to meet with the Russian Evangelistic Ambassador in Portland, Oregon. Since we didn't have the money to go, we tried to sell the jewelry given to us by Rainbow while we were in Santa Fe. So we worked our way to Monroe, Louisiana and then on to Portland.

We arrived with only $4. We were given lodging in Salem, Oregon by dear friends who owned a Statehouse Bed and Breakfast. This was where we stayed those months we were in Oregon the year prior. By the time we arrived in Oregon we only had two days to get our tickets; still no money came. We prayed, "Lord, we've done all we know to do, now it's up to You."

The truth is, when the invitation came to go to Russia, we never sought God's will on it as we were so excited and just headed in that direction. We must be led by the Spirit.

We had been there three days and just didn't know what to do when we received a call from our dear friends, Pastors Ed and Gerri Deboard.

We loved these people so much. They told us they felt God had brought us there for a reason and that we should stay with them. They had a room over their garage that had a bathroom and a couch that could be made into a bed, and we could eat with them. We were so happy. "Okay, Lord, now what?"

The next day we drove into Portland and saw the streets loaded with runaways, punk rockers, gangs, drunks, drug pushers, drug addicts and prostitutes. We decided to do the only thing we knew how to do. That night we made sandwiches and, along with the Deboards and some on-fire people from the church, hit the streets. At first, the people were a little hesitant but as time went on they began to watch for us. The Street Reach of Portland, Oregon was birthed.

In order for the people on the streets to recognize our witness teams we had aqua tee shirts made that said "Street Reach of Portland, Oregon" on the front and "Jesus Loves You" on the back. Before long this ministry really grew. Since we had no support we again had to believe God for everything.

The months of putting Street Reach together were very trying times. Many times, the desire to quit would come on us. Then we heard Pastor Hawthorne preach a sermon based on Titus 1:5. Titus had told Paul that he wanted to leave Crete, but Paul said to Titus, "Don't quit, stay in Crete." Read it for yourself; it is so good.

Praise God, victory is on the way! The battle is the Lord's. He is never too late. God is going to turn it around. Keep standing. DON'T QUIT! Help is on the way. Give God praise. Praise Him continually and DON'T QUIT!!

Friday Nights

Every Friday night at 8 p.m. the witness teams would meet at the church on the Street Pizza Parlor and have a time of warfare prayer, praise and worship. Then at 9:00 p.m. we would hit the streets. We would divide into two groups and stand at the major intersection of 82nd and Powell or up on 122nd. Russell would hold up the 10 foot cross and Randy Coy, his huge "Jesus Loves You" sign, as others passed out tracts. When the cars stopped for the traffic light these brave warriors for Jesus ran into the street and passed out tracts as fast as they could. It was a bold witness and lives were touched by it.

Some said, "Praise the Lord!" While others said, "Satan rules." Some rejected the tracts and threw them back at us, but the majority of the people, both young and old seemed very happy for them and read them.

Homeless Camp Hope

Russell ministered to the leader of a homeless camp hidden down near the Ross Island Bridge. Jim, their leader, said the sinner's prayer and asked if we would come to the camp. First Russell and I carried food and jackets to the camp. We had found favor and now others would go with us. Randy Coy gave them a dog, which opened still more doors. On Saturday morning we took witness teams in there and did praise and worship led by Lee Jones and they loved it. People like Patrick, Russell, Lee or myself shared the Word and our testimonies. Then we all just talked to them. We carried bread and food to them every week.

Laundry Ministry

On Saturdays, Russell, Randy Coy and I visited the camps and picked up their dirty laundry and took it to the Laundromat and returned it to them clean and folded. We had found that the homeless would more readily attend church when dressed in clean clothing. We saw them taking more pride in themselves, also, when they were clean shaven and bathed, which is no easy accomplishment, as they must bathe in the river or a nearby fountain.

Then, on Sundays, we would load up as many as we could get in our van and take them to church. We would make them all go to the restroom before going into church, then march them all in together and seat them on the first two rows. My heart would leap for joy as they would go up for prayer. Many of the church people would go up and pray with them and love on them.

After working with Jim and the people there for almost two months, we saw many changes in their lives. Weekly, the camp looked better and better. They began to take pride in their camp. Much to our surprise, early one Saturday when we went down there, just as we came down the path into the camp, the first thing we saw was a huge cross 10' x 4'. Nailed to the cross was a prayer list of needs they asked God for: simple things like soap, tooth brushes, tooth paste, tents, blankets, Coleman stoves, lanterns, coffee pots, flatware, dishes, etc. On the tree next to the cross was a sign with a cross on it that read, "CAMP HOPE—This is a Christian Camp."

I began to weep, seeing how the Good News Gospel and the love of Jesus shown through His people, can change even the hardest hearts. These were tough guys—murderers, thieves, drug addicts, etc., but God changed them! That Sunday when we went to church, without telling anyone what was on the list, on the altar was everything except an axe. Praise God! Russell and Jim checked off the list. What a tangible sign to them of how God answers prayer! They talked about it for weeks.

That same morning Greater Portland Assembly of God gave us a bus to use. What a Sunday it was! God had been dealing with Jim's heart. On Sunday he went forward to say the sinner's prayer again. He told Russell that he was a hustler and when Russell gave him that first sandwich, he saw a meal ticket for the camp. Russell and I knew this, however, but we loved him and treated him as though he was saved and prayed continually for him. By this constant love shown to him or Russell saying, "Jim, as a Christian, you can't talk like that," or, "That's not right," he was convicted. We saw changes daily.

In the camp, there was a 14-year-old female prostitute. She was against everything that had to do with God. Almost every word coming out of her mouth was foul. The others would tell her not to talk like that in front of us. Her name was Spice. She was full of demons and liked it. She would say she was going to hell with the devil, but I knew God could change this hard heart!

One of the greatest victories in the camp was Pat, a skin head. When we first met him, he called himself, "Leviathan." He said it was a Bible name. We looked it up and it was another name for Satan. When he gave his life to Jesus, he immediately changed his cultic pants and his name. Pat, I believe, will be an evangelist. He opened doors for us to minister to other skin heads! He, along with others, asked for Bibles. One morning when we went down to the camp, there he was, reading the Word. We were able to get him into Teen Challenge.

There was a 14-year-old boy, runaway, a male prostitute. We prayed; he must get off the streets or he would be dead! He was a wild kid! Jim said he didn't know what to do with him and Spice. It was much too dangerous for them out on the streets, but they were not a good influence on the camp either. We also had a former "Crip" gang leader from Los Angeles, Willy. He gave his life to Jesus. There are so many stories to tell that these pages could not hold them all. Just pray for these folks—for their protection.

Jim, the leader of Camp Hope, took us to a riverbank camp under the bridge. They were eating ketchup and bread sandwiches. So we carried them food and bread.

War Zone

Skid row as some may know it, on Burnside. Saturday after we had been at the camp we passed out around 200 sandwiches to the homeless, drunks, drug addicts, prostitutes, etc. This is a hard area. Many times it is so discouraging to talk to drunks, but when you see changes in their lives, or you see them on one of the programs and doing well as a result of your helping and praying for them, it is worth it all.

There was such a need there. Some weeks, we would go out and everyone we prayed for would break down and cry. They would say to us, "Why are you making me cry?" It is the power of the Holy Ghost. Many have said the sinner's prayer, but we would still see them there week after week. As we continued to pray for them, however, I knew God would completely deliver them and set them free.

Many times the drug dealers or prostitutes would come to us and tell us that they wanted off the streets or wanted to get into a program, but most places of value were full. I felt so helpless, when there was no place to send them. It was really good when they saw us in our jade green tee-shirts because they had learned that we were their friends and that they could trust us. It is so surprising what a sandwich and a kind word can do. Isn't it wonderful to know that Jesus loves even the unlovely? As we show them the love of Jesus we will see lives changed.

One day a tough guy said to Russell, "Get that wheel off your cross." His anger built toward Russell just because he had a wheel on the cross. He said, "I'm gonna knock you flat!" As he drew his arm back to hit Russell, the power of the Holy Spirit came upon me immediately. I jumped between him and Russell and said, "Wait, you can't hit him, he's my husband," and smiled at him. He stopped and began to laugh. He said, "No way!" I said "Yes, he is." It struck him so funny that he just laughed and laughed. Now I know what the Word means when it says He uses the foolish things to confound the wise. This guy became putty in my hands. Praise the Lord! We witnessed to him but he never gave his life to Jesus, however; no one could ever touch us on that street because he was a gang leader and we had his protection. I'm still believing for his salvation.

One day Randy, Russell and I were witnessing to a Vietnam veteran who was stoned out of this mind. Russell said something to him and he went straight for Russell's throat. Randy and I tried to pull him off and I said, "You loose him in the name of Jesus." He would stop and go after Russell's throat again. Randy and I continued to pull him off, using the name of Jesus.

At the same time there were five Mexicans standing there whom we had just fed. They began to yell something in Spanish and the man stopped and talked back to them in Spanish and went after Russell's throat for the third time. This time, those five guys began to beat this man up and acted as protection for Russell. Now, we had to stop that fight; finally we were able to separate everyone.

Russell told the Mexican that everything was okay, and the man who had tried to choke Russell stood behind him. We then took this man over to the mission and put him into their detox program.

Weeks later, when we were at the mission this same man was there all cleaned up and working in the kitchen. His face radiated with the love of Jesus. When Russell told him what happened, he had no remembrance of the incident. From that time on we were treated like kings and he gave us special food for the ministry.

Saturday Market

Some of the witness teams chose to go through the Saturday market. Many tracts were passed out, people prayed for and new friends made. Lives were changed as a result.

Bread Ministry

We started at 8:00 a.m. on Monday, Wednesday and Friday to collect the bread. We would fill the van with bread and sweets, approximately 2,500 loaves a week. It was hard work, but it was worth it as we delivered bread to nine ministries including poor families, our homeless camps and the Russian immigrants. The Russians say it is manna from heaven.

Praise the Lord! Many times after our bread runs when there was bread left, we would watch for people in poor areas and give them bread. What an open door for ministry!

Food and Tract Ministry

After our bread pick-up and delivery at 2:00 on the same days, we would go and pick up crates of food from the mission. What a blessing this was to the many people who received it. We also passed out 300–500 tracts a week.

TV Program Street Reach

Praise the Lord, through Portland Cable Access, we were able to produce a TV program called, "Street Reach." These programs showed what was happening on the streets and what other ministries were doing to reach out. New Age, Satan worship, cults, homeless, hurting people, etc. were covered in those programs. There were many street scenes, as well as action shots of people being prayed for and getting healed on the street. Those programs challenged people to be bold witnesses for Jesus. If someone didn't know Jesus, we prayed that they would receive Him as their Lord and Savior, as there was a salvation message at the end of every program.

What the Devil Meant For Bad, God Will Turn To Good

On a Saturday evening our van was broken into and all our praise and teaching tapes and our tape player, camera, film, VHS tapes, duffel bag and, most important, Randy Coy's camcorder were taken. The three of us had been out shooting all day for our TV programs. All that footage was taken. We agreed together that everyone who came in contact with those items would get saved, and that they would listen to the music and teaching tapes and get ministered to by the Holy Ghost.

The devil may have stolen what belonged to God but we would put an even greater hurt on his kingdom and snatch souls from the realms of hell into the kingdom of heaven. This was a great loss to us, but perhaps these people who stole our things would have never had anyone pray for them if they had not done this. So, we were believing God for their salvation and we forgave them.

As the months went on we so much desired to have a building to bring the people off the streets and raise them up in the things of the Lord. I would be so discouraged when one of the prostitutes would come up to me and say "Look Mom, I'm clean!" She would stretch out her arms and show me that she had no fresh needle marks but a few weeks later, she would be all strung out again. The camps were working pretty good and we were seeing changes but to really work these people back into society we would have to get them off the streets. We spent many hours in prayer about a building.

One day I saw a building that seemed perfect. It was right off Burnside Bridge, facing Burnside. It was a great location. It had 100,000 square feet. The owner found favor with what we were doing and said that we could have it for trade if we would fix it up. We were so excited.

We drew up the plans and began to seek out oil grants. He gave us the key and we had an open house and dedicated the project to the Lord. When the city fathers heard of what we were doing, they threatened the owner.

He was in the middle of building a high rise and they said that they would stop his permits if he allowed us to continue with this project. The city did not want another street program. They would send fire trucks and hose out the camps under the bridges. However, they never touched our camp because it was hidden in a wooded area and was hard to find.

At one time they threatened to come in, take everything and dismantle the camp, but we called out the news, and after covering the story, we were left alone. The owner of the building came to us and said, "I can't let you have this building, however, they can't stop me from leasing it. So I will need what I would regularly charge $50,000 a month rent." All looked so hopeless.

After that we sought after many buildings, but each time, one door after another would close in our faces. We even went so far as writing four different leases on four different buildings. Each time everything seemed to be a "GO!"—then when we prayed over the leases, God would shut the door.

We were asked to help other TV stations around the country, but we said, "No," because we believed God had called us there. So we worked with what we had until a building would open to us. Quite a large ministry had been birthed.

We had had an emergency call from Monroe, Louisiana to help them with their TV station, as the owner, Pastor Charles Reed, had had emergency surgery and needed our help. We said we could not come at that time because we were just starting this ministry and we felt that we should not leave at this time. Pastor Charles had been so good to us so many times, so this kept weighting on me.

Looking over all the heavy load of what was happening there, I began to look at who we could place in charge of the different facets of the ministry. I was able to put different people in charge of various areas of ministry and Street Reach could keep going without us for a short time. So this is how we prayed. If we get a building or a place of our own to live in before September 21, we would stay; however, if this didn't happen before that date, we would leave October 1. We prayed this for a month.

What the devil meant for bad, God will turn to good! We believe that where God guides, He will provide.

After praying for a month for direction and no open doors for a building or a place for us to live, we left for Monroe, Louisiana. The financial struggle had been so hard; we had to believe daily for gas and money for other needs. I remember that all we had sometimes was change that someone had given to us.

One Saturday we had to wash the clothes for the camp and went all day without any money until late that afternoon someone gave us $4. We praised the Lord and went and washed the homeless folk's clothes.

We had lived with the Deboards for five months and felt it wasn't fair to them to keep us there any longer. They were so kind to us. If this was going to be a permanent ministry for us in Portland, we felt that God could provide us a home of our own. Since nothing opened up to us we turned each facet of the ministry over to other leaders and left for Monroe.

We drove to the outside of the Portland city limits; it was pouring rain when all of a sudden our van began making a strange noise and we began to lose power. We pulled over to a gas station. The man said that just to check to see what was wrong with the van would cost us $35. We sat and talked about what to do. Charles Reed had sent us money but it was only enough to make it to Louisiana. We decided we had to just pray and trust Jesus and go. There just wasn't enough money to have it fixed, so off we went. The power wasn't great but we just believed that God was going to help us make it.

We did okay until we went through the mountains in Colorado. I was driving up a mountain and we were losing power. Soon it dropped down to about five miles an hour and Russell jumped out of the van and tried to push it. He was saying, "Van you can make it!" It was so funny just watching him. Then the van died—dead!

We flagged down help and AAA came out to help us. Ever since our car blew up in the desert we have carried AAA Plus. This was good for 200 mile towing. What a blessing it was for us because we used it regularly. The AAA driver told us it was about 100 miles to the top of the mountain outside Denver and from there on it would be downhill all the way. So he pulled us to the top of the mountain and gave us a short push, and down the hill we went. The van started up and we drove into the parking lot of the TV station in Monroe, Louisiana where the van died.

This time when the mechanic checked it he said there was no way we could have driven the van from Portland, Oregon. We were operating on only two pistons and when he went to take them out they all crumbled. Then when he checked the radiator it wouldn't hold water and the water he put in ran out everywhere. He said, "It's a miracle!" Only God could have kept this van together for us. That's the only way we could have made it. Praise the Lord! I don't know how people can live without God. He's our everything!

Bear Wrecker in Monroe, Louisiana, has been such a major blessing to us. They have taken such good care of our vehicle over these many years, at no charge to us. After seeing how we came into town, they said that it's got to be God and they were blessed to help us! Thank You, Jesus!

When we called Charles and told him that we were coming, it really blessed him. Monroe is a dark place; there are so many cults and Satan worship is strong there. That's why the enemy had attacked the TV station so much.

One night, a year prior, one of the pastors had been hosting the programs and his wife had just taken their two sons and another boy out to their van. She came back into the station to pick something up when one of her sons came back into the station, bleeding badly. Someone had come and cut up all three boys and one of their sons was killed. Charles Reed, the manager, had suffered a physical attack in which he had almost lost his life.

The TV station blew up two klystron tubes at a cost of $50,000 each if purchased new. That's a heavy burden for any TV station.

We had left one war zone to go into another. It takes much spiritual warfare to win those battles.

God's Special Blessing

The weeks we spent in Monroe, God truly blessed the station. While Charles was ill, the finances dropped and they put the studio into a small room to save on lights and electricity. When I walked in, it looked like a funeral parlor. "This has got to go," I said. So that night we moved back out into the big studio. We began to take our authority and to break bondages.

Soon, the finances began to pour in. Russell built a new set and we gave the station a new look. God gave us a lot of fun ideas where we could involve the people. One weekend we had a 55-hour telethon, going straight through from Friday night to Sunday night, to raise the money needed. We had a jail where we arrested people and they had to earn money to get out. We had a cake auction and auctioned off many other goods that were brought in; we also had a flea market. All of this live for 55 hours! We were so tired when it was over but we reached out goal. Praise the Lord! It was a great boost to the station.

We were to leave Monday morning for Florida, but our van still wasn't fixed. So we stayed an extra week. In the middle of the week I received a call from a pastor friend and he invited us to speak in his church on Sunday evening. "By the way," he said, "Arthur Blessitt will be preaching." I said, "Did you say Arthur Blessitt?" He said, "Yes! I thought that might make you happy." To meet Arthur would be like meeting the Queen of England. It was my greatest heart's desire. I could hardly believe my ears. I was also told that we could do an interview for TV with him if we so desired. I said, "Yes, yes, yes!!!" Pastor Tommy told me Arthur was scheduled to be there two weeks from then, but because of a schedule change he would be there this Sunday. I knew it was God!

I couldn't quit praising God. Just think, Arthur Blessitt! I had read so much about this wonderful man of God and now, through a miracle of God, I was going to meet him face to face! We arrived hours early. It was getting closer and closer to the time of the service, when all of a sudden I felt a tap on my shoulder and I turned around and there he stood.

He said, "Hi Dorothy, I'm Arthur Blessitt." All I could say was, "It's you, it's really you!" With that he hugged me and said, "I'm so glad to meet you." There was an instant bond. Then I was blessed to meet his wife, Denise, a great woman of God. She is full of so much joy. It was a red letter night in our lives. I have never felt so loved in my life.

When Arthur talks to you, it's you and Jesus. He doesn't talk to you and look up at what's going on in the room. He looks in your eyes and gives you 100 percent. Russell and I have never met a man so full of Jesus. When he talks it all Jesus and what Jesus has done.

God couldn't have given him a better wife than Denise; they are so in love with each other. She walks the cross with him or drives ahead of him setting up lodging, etc. She's been a God-send for him.

Arthur has been a real role model for us when it comes to evangelism and humility, staying real with people. We love them both so much.

God's Provision

Two years ago when our car blew up in New Mexico, a dear lady gave us some gold jewelry valued at $3,800, and said that one day this would buy us transportation. We tried time and time again to sell the jewelry to buy a van or to buy our tickets for Russia, but we never could find a buyer. We knew that if we were to go back out on the road we would have to have a different van, as our old van just could not make another trip across the country.

We came into agreement according to the Word of God and asked for a Dodge Ram, burgundy and silver, maxi van, with comfortable seats, one we could be proud of, and not look like shabby poor Christians.

Over Christmas we looked at one van after another, but nothing ever worked out. One week before we were to go back out on the road, we picked up a paper and found a van priced at $5,800 but was marked down for a weekend special to $3,999. We went to look at it and it was exactly what we wanted. We told the dealer we would take it for $2,500 and that we would come in Wednesday to close the deal. What he didn't know was that we didn't have the money. We prayed and came into agreement. Wednesday came and we still did not have the money.

So we went to the dealer and told him all we had was this jewelry. He told us that someone had come in and bought the van and they were just waiting to clear the financial end. We never changed our confession; we told the dealer that that was our van and that God would provide the money for it.

At that point we committed it entirely into God's hand. I had tried to sell the jewelry and couldn't. So now it was up to Him. On Sunday night, I had completely forgotten about the van, when a friend wanted me to show the jewelry to a lady in our church. I just happened to have the jewelry in the van. Praise God, the next thing I knew, we were given a check for $2,500. I told them to make it out in the dealer's name. I don't know if those dear people wanted the jewelry, I just believe they were being obedient to what God had told them to do.

Soon I was handed more money and more money. God poured out his blessings on us that night in such a magnificent way.

We went back to the dealer and our van had a sold tag on it. They told us someone else had come in and purchased the van for $2,999. I gave him the check for $2,500 and said, "This check says that is our van. God provided this and I know that is our van." After about an hour or so a miracle happened! The owner of the lot came out to us and said they had worked it out and we could have the van for the $2,500 plus tax. Praise the Lord!

God's Word works. Where two agree as touching anything, they shall have whatever they say. Children of God, let's learn to take God at his word.

To finish the van story, later that day we were given beautiful seats that reclined and a couch, all brand new, for a fraction of their cost. We were given materials to refinish the inside that matched the seats perfectly. We were also given carpet for the floor (Philippians 4:19).

We had decided to give our old van to another ministry. Just as we did, someone called and offered us $800 for it, but we knew that God wanted us to give it away. When we called this minister, he said he had been praying for a van. Praise the Lord, we didn't allow the devil to steal our blessing.

The Flood

In April we were able to help move TV-39 in Monroe, Louisiana to an area in West Monroe that was a much safer area. Actually it was where the tower and transmitter site had been for KARD TV-14, but they moved to a new location and sold their station to TV-39 at a good price. It was an exciting move.

Russell built beautiful new sets and I produced and hosted programs to help them through this move. We had just moved in and a few days later we went right into a telethon. It was so exciting. People came out of the woodwork. Everyone was happy about the move. Russell was given a room where he put all his tools and I had a room where I put all our clothes, shoes, tapes, prints, etc. That room also served as my office.

We had told Charles we would stay a month or so to help him through the move. We had been in there for three wonderful weeks. We left for the weekend to go back to Florida to take care of some business. Since we were only going to be gone for a few days, we left everything at the station.

We had been in Florida only a day when we got a call informing us that the station was five feet under water. That meant my painting of "The Bride," thousands of prints, all our clothes, Russell's tools, and everything of value that we owned was under water. I said, "Father, help us!"

My main concern was for "The Bride" print. I just asked God to protect it. It was a week before the water went down enough for us to go in. What a mess, so many things gone. We were able to take the painting of "The Bride" over to a local frame shop where we carefully washed off all the mud from the painting. Then we were able to carefully separate the painting from its backing. It took hours of tedious work, but we did it. The painting was saved.

The next thing I wanted to save was all my scrapbooks. Every year since we began the ministry I've kept a diary and photograph scrapbooks. I lost most of the diary because of the ink that I used, but I was able to save most of the pictures by carefully removing them from the scrapbooks, washing them and drying them. The clothes and shoes God would just have to replace.

It's been one attack after another against this station, but Charles never gave up. We knew he needed help so we continued to stay on—snakes, mud, mildew odors—what a mess it was. It seemed never ending. The brighter side was that I had never liked the way the station was decorated. So now I had my chance to change things.

Russell built a make-shift studio, then began to strip down all the offices and hallways while I spent days on the phone trading advertising for carpet, lumber, mirrors, wallpaper, paint and furniture.

I would pray for favor. We were so blessed to be able to trade advertising for everything we had need of. When I called the lumber companies they all said, "No." I called one particular company three times.

When I saw that the company was advertising on a secular station, I called the owner again for the fourth time and said, "I saw your advertisement on a secular station but I wanted you to know that we have a great viewing audience who are Christians and who watch only our station, so they will never see your advertisement on that other station."

I told him that he needed to advertise with us. He said, "I know that's right, because all my mother watches is your station."

I said, "Mark, you must be a Christian. We need you to come down and give your testimony." He said, "I don't think you will want my testimony now." I said, "Mark, you mean to tell me you don't know Jesus? If I were you, I wouldn't take another breath without Him, especially in the work you do, because you could be killed in an accident and die without Jesus. That's the craziest thing man, you've got to get your heart right!"

He said he knew that I was right but he just wasn't ready. I had another call so I told him I just wanted him to know I was going to pray for him and, with that, I hung up. Within minutes, he called me back and said that I could have all the lumber I needed. Praise the Lord!

I had made a deal with the carpet people and on the day that it was ready to be laid, I called and told them that we were ready for the carpet. They told me the owner changed his mind. I said, "He what?!" I asked if he was there. They said that he was, but he was tied up and couldn't come to the phone. I hung up and told the people at the station that I was going to go get the carpet. When I got there the owner still was tied up, so I said, "I'll wait." I waited until closing time. When they were ready to close I said, "I'm not leaving without being able to talk to the owner."

He finally came out to talk to me. I said, "We made a deal, what's up?" He said that he had been hurt by so many Christians that he really didn't want to do it. I said, "When I give you my word, it's my word. I promise you, you will never get advertising like I'm going to give you." So he agreed. Praise the Lord!

That night when I got on the air I talked about how wonderful he was and what all he had done for us. I asked the people to get on the phone and call him to thank him, after all it was their station and they should be the ones saying "thank you" as well as us. The next day the carpet company was flooded with calls. From that day to this we have been blessed to have all the carpet we have needed. God is so faithful.

When we were finished it was beautifully decorated. People were so proud of it.

I had the best role model for excellence in ministry in my pastor, Tim Gilligan. We should have the best, after all, we are King's kids. Everything we do should be our very best. Look at King Solomon's temple. Nothing was spared.

Lisa's Chickens

While in Monroe, we planned a day in the park for the TV Station. We scheduled gospel singing groups, games, etc. We also planned to sell barbeque chicken.

Now the problem was, there was no money for the purchase of the 500 chickens needed. I put Lisa in charge of getting the chickens. She came to me and said she couldn't get anyone to give us that many chickens. I told her to write on a piece of paper a petition to the Father asking and thanking Him for those 500 chickens and place it on her refrigerator. Every time she saw that paper she was to thank Jesus for her chickens. I promised her that God would honor His word.

She later told me that when she first started doing this she thought I was crazy and had no faith that it would work, but because she knew I would ask her if she was thanking God for those chickens, she did it. Soon it became real in her heart and the Tuesday before we needed the chickens a man called and gave her all she needed.

You must exercise your faith. Believe you receive when you pray and thank God continually, and you will see it done (Mark 11:24).

Nothing's Too Hard For God—
Arizona Trip

We were asked to go to Lake Havasu, Arizona to help raise up a TV station and walk the cross. While we were driving through the desert, all of a sudden we heard this awful noise. Russell saw our back tire take off across the road. He was able to pull the van to the side of the road.

We jumped out and saw the back of our newly painted van was on fire near the right wheel which was right beside the gas tank. The wheel had frozen up and snapped off. Several semi-truck drivers pulled off the road in front of us, and one behind us. Quickly they came running towards the van with fire extinguishers. They were able to put the fire out.

All the time this was going on, Russell was standing near the front of the van with his hands in the air just praising God. The truckers asked me if he was okay. I said, "Yes, he's praising God; this is His van, not ours, and it was His problem, not ours." They just shook their heads in amazement. They said that Someone was watching over us, because the van should have flipped when the tire came off or it should have blown up with the fire.

I said, "It's the angels that watch over us." They proceeded to tell us how bad all this was. It would need a new rear end, on and on they went. We said that Jesus would take care of it! We really were able to witness to them. They called an AAA dealer to pick us up.

By the time they got there it was almost dark. They towed us to the place where we spent the night. We prayed and said, "Lord, we only have $132 to our name, You're going to have to take care of this for us." We went to sleep in complete peace. The next day I asked the Father for wisdom.

Lake Havasu was about 70 miles away. I looked through the phone book and found several repair shops in Lake Havasu. I asked the Father which one to call and He led me to a particular one. The owner was wonderful and said, "Bring it here and let me see what we can do."

So we had AAA haul us to Lake Havasu. We witnessed to the driver all the way. After looking the situation over, he said we would need a new rear end. Even if we could find a used rear end, it would cost us $900 to $1,200. He said he would see what he could find.

When he mentioned a used rear end, I remembered Bear Wrecker in Louisiana. They told us if we ever broke down to let them know and they would do their best to help us, so Russell gave them a call and told them what we needed. They said they would check and see what they could do.

The next day we received a call. They found a rear end that would work and they worked it out with a truck line to have it brought out to Phoenix, Arizona all at no cost to us. What a mighty God we serve!

There was a man in Lake Havasu who said he would gladly pick the part up for us in Phoenix because he had to make a trip there. Now it was up to Marty the repair man. He also was wonderful. His normal charge for repairing a rear end was $525 and he cut the price down to $125, which we could pay. What a blessing from the Lord!

By the way, he not only repaired the rear end, he put rims on as well as new brakes and made other minor repairs. Just because of his love for Jesus. At Christmas he sent us a check for $200.

Praise the Lord!

1,000 Miles Plus—Walk in a Miracle

Our walk began in Shipshewana, Indiana as we headed for Detroit, Michigan. From there we traveled to Gettysburg, Pennsylvania on our way to Portland, Maine. Our plans were to walk through Canada, up the St. Lawrence, and then down through the New England States, but when we weren't able to get the cross into Canada, we saw God's hand at work in the route we took. It was awesome! There were two other members to the team—Randy the driver, and Ruthie, the coordinator.

We said, "Lord, we are never going to ask for any money, clothes or food." We did ask churches to help us with lodging, and daily, God supplied all our needs. These next pages will be inserts taken from my diary. When you walk the cross, every day brings a new experience. Many pages could not hold all that happened but here are some of the highlights.

The second day of the trip, I told Russell I felt a heaviness. Soon after, there was a horse and buggy that passed us going the other way. It wasn't but a few minutes later that we heard tires squealing; we looked to see what was happening. The buggy was in the ditch, with cars all over the road. It wasn't very much longer that we heard the squeal of tires again, only this time, cars were all around us. We were walking on the outside of the white line; one car passed us in the ditch while three others were all over the road around us.

It was like the devil tried to kill us, but God sent His angels to protect us. From that time on, I knew we had the angels surrounding us. Believe me, we needed them on US Highway 1 when we walked through New Jersey, New York and the New England states. We were told later, that in the area where we were almost hit, there were many accidents. So we began to pray and pull down the principalities that ruled over that area.

The second night on the road, we were blessed to stay at the home of Corneal and Lena Weldy, an Amish family who gave up family, church, and friends to know Jesus. When they gave their lives to Jesus and received the baptism of the Holy Spirit, they were shunned by their family, church, and friends.

One day Corneal went to buy a hog from an Amish man who was going to sell it to him until he found out who he was and that he had left the church. Their lives had to be completely changed. They could no longer talk with their sisters, brothers, or parents. They had a very high price to pay. As the years have gone on, they have become missionaries to the Amish. Slowly, they are seeing some come to Christ. Being with them was a wonderful time of encouragement. There is a cost for discipleship but there are also rewards for sacrifice (Mark 8:34–38; Luke 9:23–26; 14:25–33; Matthew 19:27–30).

The next night we stayed in the house of Barb and John Hooley. Pastor Orvin Hooley, his father, ordained my father at the age of 18 to pastor a church. So this was also a special time for us. John, as a teenager and young man, knew the call of God was on his life, but ran as hard as he could the other way into the ways of the world. He became an alcoholic and was big into Arabian show horses. His father, mother, and wife never quit praying for him and believing God for his salvation.

One night he went to a Full Gospel Businessmen meeting, and got saved and baptized in the Holy Spirit. He would read his Bible with a pipe in one hand and a glass of wine in the other, but through his hunger for the Word, God cleaned him up and changed his life completely. Today he's an associate pastor and is preaching.

When you lead someone to Jesus, don't fill them with, "You've got to quit doing this and that," but rather, like John, turn them onto the Word of God and let the Holy Spirit do the cleaning up. As the Word gets into their hearts and they fall more in love with Jesus, you will see the change.

Whenever you begin a long walk it always starts out with leg cramps and blisters. Our legs had bad leg cramps and there were many blisters on our feet. We stayed in the home of Joe and Judy Jacobs and before we left the next day, they gave me a Jacuzzi that could be used in any tub. It made our legs feel so much better. What a gift of love!

There were always those deterrents that would come to try to get us to quit those first weeks; be it the weather, leg cramps, blisters or lack of strength.

This day a policeman came out to the road and said that we had to get off the road. Russell said that the law says we can walk anywhere on the side of the white line on a secondary road and, besides that, we were wearing our orange jackets so he had no cause to get us off the road. He continued to insist that he was told we had to get off. I proceeded to pull out the news coverage and said, "I guess you haven't heard of us. We are being covered by all the major news networks because we are on a pilgrimage walking the cross through every state in the nation."

With that he took off his cap and sort of brushed back his hair with his fingers. Then he said, "Sorry, I didn't know, where are they?" referring to the news people. Before all was said and done, he gave us his card and said, "If you get into any trouble here in Michigan just give me a call, I will help you out. You can use my name anytime." He then handed us money to help us on our way. Thank You, Jesus, for Your wisdom and favor.

A semi-truck driver stopped and, with tears in his eyes, said he had given his life to Jesus during the Saudi Arabia War. Seeing the cross, he was convicted because he had back slid and he wanted to pray and give his life back to Jesus. The power of the cross brings conviction.

A man named Mark came out to the cross and, as he walked toward us you could tell he loved the Lord, but there was a heaviness about him. He told us that his wife forbids him to read the Bible, or to pass out tracts. There had been times he had kept his Bible and tracts in the car and while he was at work, she would come and take them out and destroy them.

He knew God had called him to preach. He said when he saw us walking, his heart was stirred. He began to cry like a baby and he said it touched him so much to see two people who would give their all and walk for Jesus. We all began to cry. We prayed and took authority over that situation with his wife, believing first for her salvation. Weeks later we saw him again and he said that things were beginning to change. To God be the Glory!

We were walking through the Irish Hills in Michigan and it was very hot; walking up and down the hills was exhausting. Again, I was hampered with, not one, but four, blisters on my feet. Russell was much better on this walk because he would stop and give me rest times when I needed them.

We were sitting, resting at the edge of a beautiful golf course. Russell, in all the years I have known him, has never spoken about wanting to learn to golf. Probably, because we've just never taken the time off to do things like that. As we were sitting there he said, "I wish I could have someone who really knows how to play golf to teach me how to swing a club and what clubs to use when…" I said, "Russell, that's great but you don't even have golf clubs." He said, "I know, but I'd just like to learn anyway."

That night our hosts were Pastor Chad and Debbie DeWeerd, pastor of Teeumsseh Evangelical Friends Church, a Quaker Church.

Pastor Chad, a wonderful young pastor, told Russell that he had been a professional golfer when God called him to preach. This was the night he taught the men from his church how to golf and asked Russell if he wanted to go along! Russell was so happy. First, it was his heart's desire that he had just spoken that very day. Second, it showed Russell how much the Father loved him to open up that door for us to stay in that home.

Every day, we prayed for Randy and Ruth to have God's wisdom and the favor in finding us a place to stay. Usually, when they are looking for a place to stay they drove ahead to the next town. However, that day, while they were driving, Randy said, "I just feel like we should drive down this road."

It wasn't in town but he was led by the Spirit. Several miles down the road there sat a beautiful large church. It was Pastor Chad's church. We know the Spirit of God led Randy there. Pastor Chad asked us if we could stay another day; he wanted us to minister the next night at his church and he also wanted himself and his youth pastor to walk the cross with us the next day, which we thought was great. When a pastor walks the cross, I know it really makes a marked difference in his ministry.

When speaking with him after the walk, he said it made him realize that there are no comfort zones on the cross, as his shoulder hurt from the weight of the cross. "It makes one reflect on the great sacrifice Jesus made for us. I was blessed by those who waved in favor of the cross, but even those who had the degrading remarks, I know it planted a seed in their lives. For without accepting what Jesus did on the cross, they can have no peace, joy or hope. It gave us a real awakening to the streets in our town. We send money overseas, yet we forget to minister in our own hometowns. It was in the streets where Jesus walked and met the people in need, from the tax collector, to the physician, to the poor and needy."

He continued, "We, as a ministerial group, are planning to do a prayer walk from the hospital, past points of interest, industrial areas and to city hall, stopping at each point for prayer. We may just build us a cross and take it with us. It is a powerful way to witness and a real attention getter."

He finished by saying that when he was a professional golfer, it was great reaching one achievement after another. It was all the world had to offer him, but he never had real fulfillment in his life until he made Jesus his Lord. It was a powerful testimony.

That night after the service Debbie, Pastor Chad's wife, came to me and said, "Come with me, we're going shopping; the Lord told me that you need a new pair of shoes." What a blessing, because my feet had been swelling and I had four blisters that I just couldn't seem to get rid of ever since the walk began.

One day we had only enough money for food for Ruth and Randy so I gave it to them. They said, "What are Russell and you going to eat?" I told them that God would supply. It was about noon when we walked into Clinton, Michigan. At the edge of the city was a park. One of the ladies from the Clinton Women's Club came out to us and invited us to have lunch with them in the park. What a spread! While there we were asked to speak. It was a blessing.

As we walked closer to Detroit the traffic got increasingly worse. It was very humid and hot on this particular day and the sweat was just dripping off us. We didn't take the wagon because of the bad road edge and the fast moving traffic, therefore we had no water with us. We were walking country miles and needed water very badly.

There was a bar so I went in and asked for a glass of ice water. Several men in the bar asked me what Russell was doing out there with the cross. I told them. It was seed planting time. Then they questioned why I would come into a bar. I told them, "That's where Jesus would go. He loves you all so much." It was neat! I had found favor. Beside that I said, "We are thirsty and need water." After some witnessing I asked for a cup of ice water to go. The bartender went to the back and brought out this dirty cup. Russell and I just blessed it and said, "Lord, kill all the germs!" and then we drank out of it.

It was about 4:00 Saturday evening. We rested in the wide median strip under a shade tree. Ruthie and Randy were across the street making phone calls trying to find us a place to stay; we should have had a place to stay by now. They spoke to many of the churches in Detroit but one after another had an excuse why they could not provide lodging for us. Some of the excuses were: "We're having a wedding"; "We have to approve it through the board"; "We're just too busy"; and on and on it went. They spoke to close to 30 churches, showing them our promotional materials which gave us high recommendations. Still they had no time for cross bearers. All gave an excuse.

Several suggested we go to the Salvation Army. Over the years of walking the cross we have found that in the large cities like Detroit, it's not your regular denominational churches or faith churches that help with lodging but, rather, the Episcopal, Catholic, Presbyterian or United Methodist.

Randy said we should just pitch our tent right there in the median; he was very serious. He went on to say that we had no money for food or gas and no place to stay! I said, "But Randy, we have the Father. Who's our Father? Remember, our God supplies all our needs. Has he ever failed us yet?"

"No," he said. "Well then, why should He start now?" We prayed with them and told them to check out the motels. If the churches turn us down, God can have us find favor with the motels. So on they went and on we went walking, smiling and waving at the thousands of passenger cars. All that time, for at least an hour or so I kept singing "Our God is an Awesome God" and reminding the devil how faithful God was.

A carload of young people stopped and we got to minister to them. What a pleasure it was to share Jesus with them. They said, "How do you live out here? Where do you sleep?" We told them that God provides everything. While we were talking to them, all of a sudden here comes Randy with a smile a mile wide, shaking some keys. He said, "Super 8

Motel said they've never done something like this before but they'd love to be a part of what we were doing, and gave us rooms." What a blessing! It made believers out of those young people.

Then two people drove up behind Randy and said they loved what we were doing and handed us $20. Praise the Lord! We now had lodging and gas money! We walked on up the road about a half a mile and a lady named Marty stopped and handed us four meal tickets. Praise the Lord for His total provision!!! GAS, FOOD and LODGING all within an hour!

How many times people give up and quit just before the victory comes! You must learn to put your total trust in Jesus and learn how to enter into his rest (James 1:2–4). Learn what His Word says about your situation and how to stand on His promises.

Walking into Detroit, we walked through some very rough areas. On one street corner were three prostitutes. They looked so hard. One of the girls had sores all over her. All three looked like they had been beaten time and time again. In talking with them you could feel the hopelessness, like they were stuck in a situation and couldn't get out. I prayed with them; none of them would make a decision for Jesus, but I could feel their hearts cry out. I told them there was a way out and if they would just call out to Jesus anytime, anywhere, He would help them.

I could tell the way one of them was acting that her pimp was close by. I told her she didn't have to belong to any man and Jesus could help her get out. She smiled at me as if to say, "I wish that were true." As we left we prayed and asked the Father to make a way of escape for those girls, to take the seed we had planted and let it bring forth a harvest in their lives and to send others by to minister His love to them.

As we continued to walk, we walked in front of a gospel mission. There was a man outside handing out tracts. He asked if he could walk with us. He was the best "tracker" I've ever seen. He put Gospel tracts in the phone booths, on all the cars parked along the sidewalk, and gave them to every person we passed. He told everyone to get ready, Jesus was coming soon.

A Change in Plans

We had walked to the United States / Canadian border. Our original plans were to cross the border and walk through Ontario, Canada up the St. Lawrence Seaway out to the Atlantic Ocean, down to Portland, Maine, and over to Gettysburg, Pennsylvania.

What a shock we had when we crossed over into Canada. I had gotten all the paperwork I was told I needed, however, when we arrived they made us all go to immigration. The man in charge was very much opposed to the cross and would not let us bring the cross into Canada. He said, "We don't need the cross here, so take it back where you came from." I thought to myself, *Who is this uncircumcised Philistine who should come against the things of God?* Then I spoke up and told him how we went to the Canadian Embassy in Washington, D.C., and they told us what we needed, which, we showed him and that there would be no problem! He then said we had to have $100 a day per person and a letter of invitation from each church where we would be ministering. "Without that you're not crossing my border, now get back in your van and take that cross back!" He was very angry.

So we did as we were told. We went to Greenfield Village, spread the blanket on the ground along with the maps and said, "Okay, now what?" We all agreed that if the Father wanted us in Canada, He could have had that man out to lunch.

Sometimes you may feel like you've heard from God to do a certain thing. Often times with the excitement of doing something for Jesus, we get out of His plans and over into our plans. When that happens, don't allow the disappointment of the moment, or the thinking, "I missed God," condemn you. I tell you this, God can more quickly turn the direction of a willing and moving vessel than one who sits there year after year saying, "I'm just waiting on the Lord." How that must sadden Him. Granted, there are times we have need of patience and only move as the Spirit leads, but that's not what I'm speaking about.

We prayed, "Lord, You said the footsteps of the righteous are ordered of the Lord and if we commit our ways to You that You would establish our thoughts, so Father, we do that now. We are all willing to serve You, but we must have clear direction now."

After looking at the map and looking at the different areas we could walk, we all felt at peace about going to Gettysburg, Pennsylvania and walking to Portland, Maine. We weren't going to let the spirit of "quit and give up" come over us.

Gettysburg to Portland, Maine

Driving to Gettysburg we were very short on funds. We saw a large Faith Church sign that said "Jesus is Lord" across the front of the building. I stopped and spoke to the church secretary; the pastor wasn't in at the time. I showed her our Letters of Recommendation and news clippings and told her what we were all about. We asked if they could help us with lodging or if they knew anyone that could help us. Now remember this was a very large church; she said, "No, we are all just too busy. I'm sorry, we just don't have time."

I wondered if my name was Arthur Blessitt or Kenneth Copeland if they would have time. *Lord God, help us!* I thought. As we drove on into Gettysburg we prayed that God would do a real work in that church and remove those with no compassion from positions of authority. It was getting late in the afternoon on a Friday; God would have to provide for us.

In Gettysburg God blessed us with a beautiful place to stay. It was with the Rizer Foundation. This dear old saint of God had a lovely home that, when she died, she left for missionaries or ministers of the Gospel as a place of rest. We were there four days which was a major blessing. Saturday we walked the cross through Gettysburg.

This next part I hesitate to write about because it's a girl thing, but what God did was so fantastic I just have to write about it. I had not had my monthly cycle for about two months. Since I'm always on time I thought perhaps I was pregnant. This particular day, while we were walking, I stopped Russell and said, "I think I've just started my period." He said, "No way." I had light colored pants on and was not prepared for this in any way. Besides all this we had absolutely no money, not even a quarter.

Russell said, "What do you want to do?" I said, "I don't know." Just then Russell said, "Look there's a dollar." I thought he was teasing me. He said, "No, over there! Go get it." Sure enough there was one. Then he said, "Look! There's another one!" and there was. He put down the cross and went up by the bushes and there was a third one. Then he found two quarters. About a half of a block up the street was a Wal-Mart. I was able to go purchase what I had needed and the problem was solved. Never in all our years of walking have we found dollars. Not even one. We would find many pennies, some nickels, dimes and quarters. This was Jesus meeting a very important need! We just can't stop praising Him for all His goodness.

That Sunday morning during the Sunday school period, we were asked to minister to a church congregation. These people were so receptive and hungry. Later, I knew why. The sermon was about trees. Very little, perhaps three minutes, was on how it applied to the spiritual life. It saddened and grieved my spirit. "Oh Lord, do a work in this church." They had no evening service, what a sad thing! The pastor was so kind to us. "Lord, please send revival here!" After church we were flooded with questions from these hungry people.

We walked the cross through Abbotville. It wasn't friendly to the cross. A car of four kids stopped and they asked us what we were doing. We told them and, as we spoke to them about Jesus, they laughed and mocked hilariously and took off down the road. It broke our hearts, because they weren't laughing at us but at whom we represented, Jesus. We came together in agreement for their salvation.

It's funny how God brings us across the paths of different people. We had been on "Keystone on the Line" which is a network program that goes all across America. They had us on there several times telling our story of walking the cross. We had been friends for years. They had made arrangements for us to stay in this very large church in York, Pennsylvania. It was a lovely church with a large auditorium, basketball court, showers, kitchens and classrooms. When we came in we were very tired. There was no evening meal prepared for us. We slept on mattresses which were on the floor in several classrooms. The pastor took no interest in us or what we were all about.

We stayed there for several days; we were never asked to share and challenge their people to be bold for Jesus. We read in a flyer where they were sending people, at the cost of $350, to Chicago to learn how to street witness and yet right at hand God sent two cross walkers who have been on the streets witnessing Jesus for over six years, to be a blessing to them and teach them and at no cost. Isn't it something how we can miss out on what God is doing when it's right under our noses? God help us to be more sensitive to what we are doing in these last days.

The day we walked into York, Pennsylvania, the news did an extensive story on us. The whole front page was a picture of us and our story, except for a column on each side of the picture. We have never experienced anything like that ever. The paper came out in the morning and it was awesome. Russell and I had not yet seen the paper so had no way of knowing what had happened.

As we walked, the bus drivers would honk at us, and the people in the busses would wave. Car after car would honk. One block after another we were stopped by people wanting us to pray for them. Around noon we walked by the Holiday Inn; they came out and asked if they could feed us. They not only fed us but also gave us a paper. Now we knew why we were having such a great response to the cross. All day people flooded to the cross.

That day, walking through York, was beyond anything we had ever experienced. We prayed for jobs, husbands who needed work, healings, and marriages to be healed; one girl was dating a married man and wanted advice. So many hurting people.

Do you remember the church that I spoke of earlier, the large faith church that was in Gettysburg and did not have time for us or couldn't give us lodging? After that story came out in the paper, one of the representatives of the church came out to see us and said they had a missionary house where we could stay if we needed a place to stay.

I told him that when we first arrived, theirs was the first church where we stopped and that we had been turned away and been told that they had no time or room for us. This greatly disturbed him.

The Word speaks about how some have entertained angels unawares (Hebrews 13:2). Now we are not angels, however, we must always have the compassion of Jesus and be ever ready to reach out and to help people. One never knows to whom he is reaching out.

One time we were walking through a major city and there was this lady sitting on the steps outside this restaurant. She asked me for a glass of water. At the time we weren't carrying any water on us so I told her I didn't have any. I told her that Jesus loved her and gave her a tract and walked on.

Then the Lord spoke Hebrews 13:2 to me. All I had to do was to go into that restaurant and get her a glass of water. I repented. All she had wanted was a glass of water. I'm sure as I write this to you that she was an angel. Through it the Lord has taught me not to be so busy about His work that I miss the simple needs of people. What a lesson it was for me!

Ever since I had gotten my new shoes in Michigan, I told Russell that the one on my left foot was turning my foot inward. I had gotten a huge blister on my left foot that was getting bigger and bigger and wasn't going away. By the time we had walked through York, Pennsylvania, I could no longer bear the pain.

Russell and I came into agreement for money for new shoes. Praise God, that night when Randy picked us up someone had given money for those new shoes. When you pray according to Matthew 18:19 you will always have results. I asked Randy to try on my other shoes. They fit him just perfectly. He said that he had been praying for a pair of shoes.

Pastor Ready to Quit

God opens doors for us to be able to minister in so many different churches, ministering on Sundays and two to three nights a week on the average. After walking all day it's only His strength that carried us through.

On Father's Day we ministered in a United Methodist Church of about 300 people in Pennsylvania. The anointing was so heavy that morning and when we were finished ministering, the pastor, John, got up to close the service. He tried to speak, then he stopped and began to weep. Again he tried to speak and this time he broke down and wept and wept, putting his head down on the pulpit.

He said, "My son met Russell and Dorothy, walking through the town sharing the simple Good News Gospel. He insisted that I cancel my Father's Day message and have them speak, so I did." Weeping and asking forgiveness for his weeping he proceeded, "The ministry has been so hard and today I was going to quit but God sent these two people with their simple story of faith and boldness and I've sensed Jesus like I've not known Him before!"

He said he had been job hunting and was ready to quit the ministry because of the financial struggle. Having two boys, both going to college, and being a father, he felt responsible to send them to college. Over the years the financial burden was so heavy he would preach in church and wonder in his heart if there really was a God. Now, do you want to see how God works?

That night we preached in an Assembly of God church back in York, Pennsylvania. We were telling Pastor Belch how God had moved in the morning service. He said that several pastors, along with Pastor John's wife, had been fasting and praying for Pastor John. He said, "God sent you there." Praise the Lord! We had an awesome meeting that night. Afterwards Pastor Belch had the whole church come forward to pray for us. Then he asked us to pray for him. It was a wonderful day in Jesus.

Coatsville, Pennsylvania

Before we ever walked into this town we were told it would be a dangerous town to walk through because of the crime. Isn't it sad how some people will not go into an area simply for that reason? Friends, that's where the Good New Gospel needs to be shared.

The road was hilly and winding, a pretty dangerous road for walking because of the fast moving traffic. At the top of the hill, we rounded the corner and there was Coatsville nestled in the hills, a typical steel town. We walked across a large old steel bridge and came upon two steel factories, one on each side of the road. As we were walking past the first, a large number of men who were on a lunch break were sitting around the outside of the building.

They started yelling out at Russell, mocking him. Russell said, "Okay, you guys, which one of you is brave enough to come out here and get this tract?" Pretty soon the big mouth of the group came out. There was a small group of men sitting off separately from the others. One was a black preacher and he yelled out to the big mouth, "Listen to what the man with the cross tells you, it will change your life."

The big mouth came out to Russell, mocking all the way. The others in the larger group were laughing him on and it was quite a scene. When he got to Russell he said in a quiet, more gentle voice, "Hey man, tell me what you're doing out here." Russell really ministered to him good. You could see the convicting power of God on him as his eyes welled up with tears. Russell asked if he could pray for him; he could hear his friends laughing in the background.

He said, "I believe in what you're saying but, man, I've got to go." So

Russell gave him some tracts and asked him to read one and pass the rest on to his friends. He told him that he could make Jesus his Lord anywhere and at any time, but not to delay too long. They shook hands and we watched as he went back and gave out the tracts. He said to the others, "Hey guys, they're pretty cool in what they are doing." Russell yelled out to the black preacher, "You keep on witnessing to these guys. They all act big and macho, but they all have a hunger for Jesus." Some yelled out and laughed, but you could feel the convicting power of the Holy Spirit as he moved through those men. We believed for their salvation.

We walked perhaps a half a block farther and there was another group of men on their lunch break at the other steel factory. They were standing right out by the fence. Again, the same thing happened. They were laughing and mocking, but when Russell began to speak boldly and with the power of the Holy Spirit they listened. A few took tracts, but most did not. Russell prayed out loud for all of them.

Their lunch break was over and they had to go in but, again, it was the loud mouth who had said that he was an atheist who came back out to us. He said, "I know what you're saying is right, can I have one of those tracts?" You see in both mills, it was pride and the fear of what the others would say that kept them from coming to Jesus. However, we believe that there was great seed planted in both cases and that those hard steel workers would come to Jesus.

What a ministry someone could have going out there daily on their lunch hour and being real with those guys and sharing Jesus with them. "Lord, raise up such a man!" is our prayer.

We continued to walk down the hill, walking into the outskirts of Coatsville. On the one side of the road people were standing outside their shops waiting to see the cross. On the other side where the houses were, young people were sitting on their porches, waiting for the cross to come through. It was awesome, so many hungry people for Jesus.

There were some Christians who came out and said how it blessed them to see the cross. It seemed as though it took hours to walk into

Coatsville itself. We were able to pray with so many people, everyone with a different need and problem. My eyes would be filled with tears as there was so much ministry there. What a mission field!

Walking into the center of town, you could see drug deals going on right out on the streets. Perhaps it wouldn't be so obvious to the average person but to us it was plain to see. There were prostitutes and just lots of people hanging around. When Russell and I see areas like this we just boldly go into them with the name of Jesus and the protection of His angels and His blood. We simply become their friends and share the Good News of Jesus. I can't say we had a lot of people to give their lives to Jesus, but they saw Jesus in a way they probably never did before. We passed out many tracts and even the drug lords would let us pray for them.

We were standing on this one corner and a black lady began questioning us about what we were doing. She wasn't a Christian but she said she liked what we were doing. She handed us $5; I didn't want to take it from her but she insisted. She let me pray with her, then all of a sudden some of the prostitutes, drug dealers and others just started handing us money. It was like they were taking up an offering right there on the streets for us. We said they couldn't buy their way into heaven, the gift of salvation was just that, a gift. They said, "We just like you and admire the guts you guys have in walking that cross and we want you to keep doing it!"

Isn't that something how, when the world receives a seed of life, the first thing they want to do is give, yet we have Christians in the church who won't even tithe. Read Malachi 3. If you should be one of those people, I promise you can never realize the fullest extent of the blessings you can walk in if you're not tithing.

First of all, tithing is for your sake, not God's. He wants you to learn to trust Him for everything. Money is a god to most people who aren't tithing. You object, "I can't meet my bills the way it is." I promise you that, if you get God involved in your finances, you will never lack.

Luke 6:38 says, *"Give, and it shall be given unto you; good measure, pressed down, and shaken together, and running over, shall men give into your bosom. For with the same measure that ye mete withal it shall be measured to you again."* Read what the Word says about tithing.

Secondly, in Malachi 3:11, God says that He will rebuke the devourer for your sake. That alone is enough reason to tithe. I want you to live in such victory in your life that you will have no pressure, and that you will be free to witness Jesus daily wherever you go. Worry and stress are tools of the devil to keep you bound so that you won't want to witness, because you'll be totally into yourself and your own problems.

The Billy Graham Crusade

The Billy Graham crusade was in Philadelphia on a Sunday afternoon. Randy and Russell both desired to see him. There was a Presbyterian church in Coatsville that was taking several busses to the crusade and all you had to do was sign up. We called and they had four spaces left. When we arrived at the crusade it was very hot. The sweat was just pouring off us. The stadium was packed with people. Beside us were two men who were dressed for jogging. They were wearing shorts, no shirts and smoking throughout the entire service. You could tell that they were young professional men by their mannerisms.

When it came time for the altar call, people flooded the altars. Someone came and spoke to these two young men but they said, "No." Then the Spirit of God came upon Russell and he, in his simple way, talked to them. The convicting power of Jesus fell on them. They said, "Can't we just pray with you here?" He said, "Yes, but there's something special that happens when you go forward and announce to the world you've committed to Jesus." They said, "Oh, will you go with us?" Then the other young man who had witnessed to them said that he'd love to go up with them. They said, "Okay," and up they went. I told you this story to say always be ready to speak out for Jesus. Someone's life may be on the line.

Philadelphia

We walked through West Market for about 40 blocks. Again, we were warned by people on the street that this was not a good area for two white people carrying a cross to walk through. It was a very rough area of town and probably because of the racial prejudice this was one of the worst areas we've walked through.

Once we were in it, there was no place to go but forward. So we put on a smile and passed out *Voice* magazine with a black track star on the cover that just happened to be from Philadelphia. Prior to taking this walk, someone handed us boxes of this magazine to hand out as we walked. It wasn't something planned, it was purely God.

That morning when we broke open the boxes of *Voice* magazines, those were the ones we found. Perfect for the area we walked through. You could feel the cold stares as we passed through the crowds of people. I would just say, "Hey smile, Jesus loves you." Then the smiles would come and we were able to talk to them. They readily took the *Voice* magazine.

I guess the greatest victory was when we came to an area outside a bar where there was a motorcycle gang sitting, not just on the sidewalk, but out into the streets. At first they yelled out, "You white honkies, get your white ___ out of here." They were very hateful. All we knew to do in a situation like that was to show no fear and back the devil down. So we marched ourselves right over there in the center of those guys with a smile and the protection of Jesus. We never ministered in condemnation, only showed the love of Jesus. Russell quickly handed out the *Voice* magazines as I was telling them about our walk.

Truthfully, the world is looking for people who are bold in what they believe and this brings great respect. We told them the neat things God had done for us. A lot of the time they would say, "Wow, that's a jive!" They knew what we were telling them was truth. We told them that God had a very special plan for each of their lives, but first it had to begin with their acceptance of Jesus. By the time we were ready to go, all of them, except one, said the sinner's prayer with us. Was it real? Did they really mean it, you ask?

Russell always instructs them like this, "If you really meant what you said when you prayed, then you're born again. I can't see what's in your heart, only God can!" He continues with some more instructions and always leaves them a copy of the Gospel of John. The Word says in Joshua 1:5 and Hebrews 13:5, *"I will never leave you or forsake you."* So we claim that verse for the people we pray with and believe God to continually bring people across their path to raise them up in the Word. If we have befriended a church in the area, we always turn their names, addresses, and phone numbers over to them.

A Word to Pastors and to Sheep

The cross brings conviction and awareness of one's need for Jesus in his or her life. Day after day people, just seeing the cross, will stop and say they need Jesus in their lives.

One hot day I was complaining to the Father, "Why does it have to be so hot?" when a man pulled off the side of the road and walked back towards us. His eyes were filled with tears. He said, "I just can't go on any more. Life sucks. Can Jesus help me?" We were able to share the goodness of Jesus and he prayed the sinner's prayer. Soon after, while we were still standing there a pastor and his wife came out carrying food and cold drinks for us. Right away he embraced this man and said that he would be his friend and teach him the ways of the Lord.

Pastor friend, don't ever get so big that you forget to go out and love on the common man who is hurting. The example of the Shepherd in Psalm 23 shows us how we should act as pastors. When there is one who's lost and hurting, what does John 10:11–14 say about the good shepherd? He lays down his life for his sheep. Let's never get so lifted up that we forget the needs of the people. I was raised as a pastor's daughter and there is a price to pay as a pastor.

Now a word to you who are in the flock. Don't wear your pastor out; remember he has a life and a family also. My suggestion to you if you have a problem: first, fast and pray about it for three days. Seek out for yourself what the Word has to say about your problem. Then act on the Word. If you need agreement in prayer, find a prayer partner other than the pastor to agree with you.

Now, understand if it's a real emergency, by all means let your pastor know. A pastor receiving wake up calls all night long, just because you can't sleep or because you love someone and you want prayer that they will love you back, just isn't right. Your pastor needs his rest to be able to minister effectively. Other than true life and death emergencies, a pastor should not be called in the evening or at night. Please, hear me on this, go to your heavenly Father first and trust Him to work things out for you. Your pastor will love you for it!

Read Mark 16:15–18. These verses don't just apply to pastors but to all who believe. If you're a believer these signs will follow you. Begin to operate in them. Save your pastor, so he can be an effective teacher for you and take care of those who are really hurting and may not know how to walk in the power of the Word as you do! GROW UP! Become mature in the things of the Lord!

Broken Lives Fit for the King

On our walk to North Brunswick a Russian pastor stopped to talk with us. He was so blessed at the sight of the cross going down the road. It was a real shot in the arm for us as the rest of the day was very hard walking. The traffic was extremely dangerous when we began walking up on US Highway 1. You could feel the wind of the cars and trucks as they sped by. The heat was, once again, almost unbearable and it would just sap the strength out of you. I was beginning to get a bad pain in my left breast area.

We would claim, "Father, You meet all our needs and we thank

You that Your Word says that we can do all things through Christ Who strengthens us! Thank You for Your strength and for Your healing which You have already provided for us. We declare it is being done in Jesus' name."

That night we were blessed to stay in the beautiful home of Joe and Alicia. Joe had been a stock trader on Wall Street and Alicia was the perfect host. They made us feel like kings. Joe had quite a story. He was born with two fathers, both living in the house with his mother. He had two last names. By the time he was two, both fathers were gone and the children had to fend for themselves as his mother was out chasing after men. They were very poor. His mother would force his older sister to have sex with the men she would bring home. She controlled the children by threatening suicide.

Joe tells how, because he loved her so, he thought she was serious and would fight to grab the pills away from her. On several occasions she wanted Joe to kill himself with her. At one time he was seconds away from doing it when another family member stopped them.

At the age of 13, his father tried to take his mother to court for custody of the children because of how she treated the children and how she was using his older sister. The mother immediately moved to New York City and changed her name. From that point on Joe got into a lot of trouble, he was doing every kind of drugs. By 21 he was a full time drug dealer and cocaine addict. At age 26 he had over $14,000 worth of traffic tickets so he changed his name back to his real name. Within weeks his father found him. It wasn't long after that he met with his brother whom he hadn't seen in years.

His brother had become a Christian. On that first meeting his brother gave him a Bible. Joe, thinking this was just a crutch his brother was using to help him forget their awful past, just threw the Bible down in the bathroom on the back of the toilet.

Alicia, Joe's wife, was physically and mentally abused by an alcoholic father until the age of five when he left. Then when she was 10 her mother remarried and her stepfather abused her sexually until she was 17 years old, when she became bold enough to tell the truth about what had happened to her in the past seven years. She went to college a real mess. She slept around a great deal. Drinking seemed to temporarily cover the hurts from the past. She was the life of the party on the outside, but hurting so badly on the inside. After college she went to a counselor to help her, but there just didn't seem to be any answers for her.

One night after work she was waiting at the Amtrak station when she spotted Joe. She followed him onto the train and sat directly across from him. Before she got off they were talking and she gave him her number. They began to date regularly however she was still sleeping around and not being faithful to Joe. He was still heavy into drugs.

Joe was free basing cocaine and was very heavy into drug dealing. He was ready to end his life when he saw the Bible on the back of the toilet. He picked it up and a note from his brother fell out.

The note told him to read the Gospel of John and the words in red were the words of Jesus. As he began to read, all of a sudden, the words in red were like Jesus was talking personally to him. He read and read. It was during this time that he decided to follow Jesus.

There was no one there in the room with him, and it wasn't high noon on Sunday in a church. It was only the prayers of a brother, the gift of a Bible and the moving of the Holy Spirit through the Word that he became a believer.

Never quit praying for those you love, because God has promised you that you and your whole house shall be saved.

Joe never knew about God or Jesus all the years of growing up because no one shared Jesus' love with him.

Joe began praying for Alicia. That weekend Alicia went to visit her uncle and aunt. Many times they would ask her to come over but she always had an excuse and couldn't go. All day while she was there she was so depressed. They tried to cheer her up, but she just didn't have any joy. When it was bedtime, her little niece asked her to read to her. They handed her books on Moses and Jesus. Then she read about Jesus dying on the cross. "What's this Jesus, Moses stuff, I just don't understand." With that they led her to Jesus. For 26 years she had never heard of Jesus.

When she went back and told Joe what happened he told her of his acceptance of Jesus. She then said, "Well Joe, if you're not going to do drugs anymore and I'm not going to sleep around anymore, and we're both going to live for Jesus, when do you want to get married, in the summer or in the fall?"

That fall they were married. Joe had to earn a living for his new wife, so he asked God for his wisdom. He got the lowest job as a clerk on Wall Street making $15,000 a year. Within one year he worked his way up the ladder with supernatural breaks and became a Commodity Trader on the floor. That year he made $130,000, the next $560,000, and so it went. At one point he made $5,000,000 in just a few months and lost it just as quickly.

Joe now works as a youth pastor, and on the streets. He said, "Seeing one 13-year-old boy receive Jesus is worth more than all the millions I made." Jesus and the work of the ministry is all that means anything to these two people. They have opened their home to traveling ministers and missionaries as a place of rest. They also have a ladies Bible study and an evening Bible study weekly in their home.

I told you their stories to show you that it doesn't matter what kind of background you have, be it abuse, poor or rich, when Jesus comes into your life it is truly a life change.

New York City Here We Come!

Daily we prayed for divine appointments as we walked. A wealthy businessman saw us walking the cross on this very busy road. He drove up a ways and walked back toward us. When we saw him coming we could tell he was very troubled. It was with some anger he said, "I was shaking my fist at God, because He took my son; then I saw the cross." We just listened as he broke down and cried, telling us how, a few weeks prior, his son had jumped off of one of the New York bridges, killing himself.

When he was finished I took his hand and said, "Sir, Jesus didn't kill your son. Jesus said, 'The thief—that is the devil—comes only to steal, and to kill, and to destroy: I am come that you might have life and life more abundantly.' Your son was probably listening to rock music, and doing drugs."

With that he began to sob uncontrollably. I held him in my arms and just let him cry, praying for him and loving on him. When he regained his composure, Russell and I were able to minister the love of Jesus to him. We told him he had to forgive himself; again he broke down. When he was able to let go of his own self-induced guilt he began to feel better. We were able to lead him to Jesus. When he left that place on the road, he also left the heavy weight that he had been carrying. The Power of the Blood of Jesus and a cross going down the road is awesome!

That night we drove into New York City with Joe and Bob, a man from Joe's Bible study. We went to St. Paul's Mission where we were asked to speak. This mission was located about three blocks off of Times Square and just one block up from David Wilkerson's ministry. Then we went out on the streets to Times Square to share Jesus.

We passed out hundreds of tracts to people as they shoved their way through the crowds. Pastor Dunlap, an 83-year-old dear saint of God, had been at St. Paul's for 47 years and is loved by the people who know him on the street. The next day as we began our walk through New York City we were surprised at the warm reception as we walked through Greenwich Village and up Manhattan. It was the first day of the Democratic Convention. There were newsmen everywhere looking for a story. We were able to share the love of Jesus with them and tell them of our walk. The cross had a lot of attention, and, press as well, that day.

At one point near Madison Square Garden, where the convention was held, there was a man all dressed in white with white hair and a white beard proclaiming that he was God. The ABC newsmen were there filming him. Russell walked up with the cross and said, "I don't know what this guy is all about, but he's not about the true Lord."

They interviewed Russell, and he was great! You could tell he was being led by the Holy Spirit. In the end he said something like, "Make Jesus your Lord, He loves you so much and He has a wonderful plan for your life. He will give you joy and peace like you've never known and, in the end, a home in heaven."

With the smile on Russell's face they could feel the reality of what he was saying. One newsman who covered our story said, "You both just seem to radiate!" He went on, "Many times you run into religious fruits and nuts out here, but you're both dressed clean and nice and I can tell that what you have is real!" Yes, it is! Praise the Lord!

There was a lot of ministering as we walked through New York but I guess the greatest was to the news media, because, through the Holy Spirit, we were able to show them our joy and Jesus perhaps in a way they have never seen Him before.

We walked up to Central Park and on into Harlem. Walking through Harlem was great as well. Everything was spray-painted with graffiti and was quite dirty. However, the people were so receptive to the cross and open to the Gospel. It was a powerful day! I could hear and see the angels rejoice as souls were coming to Jesus. I just know sometimes when the angels see us that they are saying, "Look! Here comes the cross right through the main streets of New York City!"

What Kind of Bicycle Are You Carrying!

Walking the cross through Port Chester, Greenwich County and Darin was quite an experience. This is one of the richest areas in the country. The cars passing were Porches, Mercedes, BMW's, Rolls Royces and Jaguars, very few if any Chevys, Fords, or Dodges. The people in the area were quite cold to the cross. A lot of them laughed, a few waved or honked, but very few stopped for ministry. They just didn't understand what we were doing.

If it happened once while we walked Connecticut, it happened fifteen times, one of the rich cars would pull up beside us and the passenger or driver would say, "What kind of new bicycle is that you're walking with?" At first I couldn't believe what they were asking. These people are so rich and smart, but they don't know that this is the cross of Jesus. I tell you, we couldn't believe our ears.

Russell would say, "Turn your head sideways, now what does it look like?" A few said, "Oh that's a cross." and would proceed to ask about what we were doing with the cross. There were others who had absolutely no idea what it could be. So I told Russell I would have to make a sign and put it on the cross so perhaps they would know. I did and they still asked. At least it was an open door to talk to them.

Please note, I know there are great Christians in Connecticut, as we met many of them. It's just that a great many of those who stopped us were so rich, yet they had no knowledge of the cross or God.

Help, Lord!

We had just walked into Connecticut and that evening when Ruth and Randy came to pick us up, they said that they couldn't find us a place to stay. We loaded up and headed down the road to find a place when, all of a sudden, we heard this awful noise. Our wheel bearing broke and the front tire was about to fall off. We had only a few dollars, not enough to get the van repaired. Now we were really at God's mercy.

I called the Howard Johnson Motel who had given us the room the night before and explained the situation and asked if we could have the room for another night. The desk clerk said that he saw no problem with it. He advised us to have AAA pull the van to the motel. By the time we got to the motel it was around 11:00 p.m. I went to check us in and the desk clerk said that he was sorry but the manager came by and said they were only allowed to give one night and that we would have to pay.

My heart sank as we didn't have any money. We all got into the van and prayed. I remembered the Comfort Inn about a half-mile up the road so I called them and found favor. They said they would help us. Our problem now was getting the van up the road with a tire that was ready to fall off. We had already used the AAA so all we could do was to pray and drive it. We laid hands on the van, prayed and went up the road. We made it, praise the Lord! We were all so tired we just went to bed thanking God for all He had done and what He was going to do.

The next morning, I woke up and prayed for wisdom concerning what to do about the van as we didn't have any way of getting it repaired. I remembered a mechanic back in New Jersey named Bob Maukey and thought that perhaps he would know someone in this area who could help us. Bob said that he would come and repair it for us. Bob and his brother brought their tools, arriving about three hours later, and offered to buy the parts needed. After working all day on the van, he took us out to dinner. What a major blessing!

The Ministry

On the streets we meet so many people. I couldn't begin to write all the stories. People from all walks of life are so hungry for something. They are trying to find happiness in riches. Yet we met a beautiful young girl driving a Mercedes, and dressed very well, who stopped and talked to us and said she felt like killing herself. Russell asked her how she would do this and she said by hanging herself.

We spent about an hour talking and praying with her. She gave her life to the Lord. We then followed up with a call to two local pastors we were involved with and asked them to please be her friend and help her grow up in Jesus. We received a letter from one of the pastors thanking us for telling him about her and that he was working with her.

At 8:00 the next Sunday morning we were asked to minister on the beach at a Presbyterian service. To our surprise there was a crowd of 300 or more people there, with their folding chairs on the beach. It was such a neat service. The youth pastor was so on fire for Jesus. After that service we were flooded by people. One man in particular stands out. He was trying to locate his son whom he hadn't heard from in years; we prayed in agreement that he would find his son. Later we received a letter stating that he had found him.

Capture the Moment

When walking, your senses become so alert to the sounds of the birds, and the woods, smells and the gentle wind blowing against your sunburned face and arms cooling you. You are more apt to notice things like a deer running through the meadow. We saw a cat that had died and his mate was lying on top of him, protecting him. It was so sad. I watched a centipede as it went round and round in circles, much like some people's lives. The New England states provided one breathtaking sight after another.

Many times Russell would go and pick some wild flowers and bring them to me. It was a very romantic time. Other times, Russell would say, "Come here." He would be holding the cross with one arm and have his other arm around me and he would say, "Let's just capture the moment," as we would stand there looking at the beauty of God's creation.

Don't get so busy in life and what you're doing that you don't take time to smell the flowers and to thank God for all the beauty He has given you to enjoy. Capture the moment!

Madison, Connecticut was such a quaint little town with its small shops, white square box houses, white picket fences and beautiful landscaping—I loved it! I could just visualize how neat it would look at Christmas, all decorated. It looked like a picture book town. Just before walking through Madison we met a policeman who was so kind to us. He kept checking on us all day long to be sure we were okay. What a refreshing change. Upon entering Madison, I dropped a glass Sprite bottle that someone had given to me. It sounded like an explosion. What a mess! That same dear policeman came to be sure we were all right and helped us clean it up. Talk about making a grand entrance—we sure did that day.

A Mess All the Way Around

At one point on this trip (I will not tell you the town or the church) we were asked to minister one evening at a denominational church. We arrived about 4:30 p.m. at the home of the pastor where we were going to have a cookout and where we would be staying overnight. When we walked into the house it looked like a place that hadn't been cleaned in years. The counters were filled with dirty dishes, pans and leftover food. There were clothes, papers, and magazines everywhere. It was such a dirty mess.

I had to think of what Kenneth Hagin said, "You can tell the condition of the church by the home of the pastor." A pastor who can't rule his home can't rule a church. The Holy Spirit has integrity and is neat and clean.

We were invited to wait in the living room. As we walked into the room, the children were watching Ninja Turtles. Our spirits just churned within us. We had to get out. Russell and I went outside and sat on the lawn and prayed.

That night in the service there were only about 50 people. The pastor and his wife were up and down, in and out, the whole length of the service. There were continuous disturbances with noisy children. That night I had bad dreams and little sleep. This pastor is dead set against Christian TV, yet his children sit and watch Ninja Turtles. He won't allow Kenneth Hagin or Kenneth Copeland materials into his church. He lets his sons watch Gospel Bill, and yet he finds fault with that. This church had been there for 20 years and is pushing around 60 people. I'm told that a year or so prior, the church was packed with over 200 people. What happened here? The church should always be moving from glory to glory.

If, in your own life you can remember the days of glowing victories, and now it seems as if there is one defeat after another, I recommend that you check your home. What are you allowing to come into it? In the final chapter you will read how you can live in constant victory.

God's Loving On Us

When you go out in full-time ministry such as a missionary, traveling evangelist or carrying a cross, there is a price that must be paid. One of mine was giving away my home of 22 years. It was a choice I had to make. The Lord gave me this scripture, *"And he said unto them, Verily I say unto you, There is no man that hath left house, or parents, or brethren, or wife, or children, for the kingdom of God's sake, Who shall not receive manifold more in this present time, and in the world to come life everlasting"* (Luke 18:29–30).

I am so in love with Jesus that I just want to be in the center of His will, and if for now that meant giving up my beautiful home, I knew, as I sought Him first, that He would take care of my heart's desires.

One Sunday I was walking on this beautiful private beach in Connecticut. You could see the sailboats and yachts as they sailed the harbor. Looking off in the distance was a small airport with private planes coming and going. Walking out to the point, there was the Atlantic Ocean where you could see the submarines. It was just a breathtaking view, and it was like God was saying, "See how I've blessed you? Had you not stepped out to trust Me with the walk, you would have never experienced this moment!"

The night before, we were asked to stay in this lovely home on a private beach area that was simply beautiful. Edna and Walter, the owners, made us feel like family. They had a big turkey dinner prepared for us and it felt like we had known them forever. It was just such a special time of God loving on us.

Over the years we have stayed in such lovely places. Many times we were given the best the people had to offer. At one time, some wonderful people gave us their bedroom while they slept on the floor. We said, "No," and they said, "What would you do if Jesus came to visit you? You would give Him your best." They had little yet they gave more than some who had much. It reminded me of the widow's mite as found in Mark 12:41–44. The friends that we have met have truly become our family. I think of that verse in Luke 18:29–30 and think of how big a family God has given us and the beautiful homes we have all over the country where we can stay at any given time. God, You are so good to us!

Early one morning, while walking on Route 1 near Charlestown, Rhode Island, a lady in a very nice car stopped beside the road to talk to me. She said, "Are you for real or are you fake? I hope you're not doing this for money." I told her that there wouldn't be enough money that could pay us to walk these many miles in the heat and the rain. We carry the cross to proclaim the love of Jesus to those who are hurting and need a Savior.

After speaking with her for a few minutes she said that she owned a restaurant about 20 miles up the road and would we please stop in and see her. We agreed to stop. When we saw the restaurant it was the loveliest old place. It was called "Wilcox Tavern." Just seeing the inside of this beautifully decorated exclusive place was such a blessing. From the moment we walked into the place we were treated like kings. The meal was fantastic (more than I could eat).

Eva, the owner, was so taken by what we were doing with walking the cross, she asked if we could pray and minister to her friend whose daughter was strung out on drugs. We were also asked to minister to others there. So we shared the plan of salvation. It was one of those special times we will never forget.

When you're witnessing for Jesus be real; you never know whose life you're touching and how it can multiply later. First impressions can be lasting impressions. Always smile and let the glory of Jesus be seen in you! This takes constant fellowship with the Father (Isaiah 60:1–3).

Even in your everyday walk it's vital that you rise up and let your light shine. This is a command, however; it is up to you to do it. Get up above your circumstances. People can see by your countenance what is going on in your life. So rise up, saints of God, and shine for Jesus.

Spiritual Warfare

Sometimes we may feel like we are going through a real spiritual battle. When I think of a dear pastor friend named Dan in North Kingston, Rhode Island our battles don't seem so bad. This is a very dark area spiritually. Near the pastor's lovely home there had been numerous satanic killings, some just a few doors down. The police say there are 19 known satanic covens, with a minimum of six members each, all within two miles of his home.

Also, in this town are stores of New Age, trolls, and many witches' covens. When Pastor Dan interviewed one of the New Age store owners, she stated that she worked right along with several of the pastors and the priest at the Episcopal Church, contacting their people by means of channeling.

We were warned about walking through that area because the year before, a young man carrying a cross was arrested. We prayed for protection and made it a point to smile and wave at all the police as we walked by them. At the very police station which had arrested the young cross bearer a year earlier, we made it a point to wave and smile at all those who were in sight and say, "Jesus loves you and He has a great plan for your life!"

Pastor Dan put up a large tent to hold a tent revival. He, personally, called over a thousand people out of the phone book. Many said they would come. The morning after he set up the tent, he saw a ring of flower petals around the tent. He knew in his spirit he had to pray. That night, besides his family, only one person showed up. He knows there are witches covens and satanic groups praying against that work.

I spoke to a converted witch. She says it is so easy to pull down a church because the witches are militant about their beliefs and many of the Christians and churches are walking in apathy. She said, "When we would find a church that we wanted to bring down, we would go out at night and walk around the church commanding, with our words, things to happen in the church. We would command division among the members, and things against the pastor. If it was a praying church with a praying pastor, it was like a wall of protection was around it and we would be powerless, but if it was a church of lazy Christians who didn't take their rightful authority and pray, we could cause church splits and that church would be more of a social gathering than one that would truly be effective for the kingdom of God."

Pastor Dan tried to get other local pastors together to pray, but with no avail. The Word says that one can put 1,000 to flight, but two can put 10,000 to flight; so he and his wife stood in the gap, praying and fighting those battles daily with the Word and in prayer. He sometimes wanted to quit and move to Florida, but he said the Spirit of God wouldn't let him. God always seems to send us to the right place at the right time to be an encouragement to pastors who are hurting.

Pastor Dan noticed our cross was cracked so he and his family built us a new one. He took our old one to put up at his church!

Providence, Rhode Island

In Providence, Rhode Island we walked right through the downtown section at noon, passing out hundreds of tracts to the businessmen and women who gladly took them. Unlike most other cities, only three people refused them.

It was also in this town that a little 8-year-old girl came to me and said, "What is that man carrying?" I said, "It's a cross." She said, "What is a cross?" I said, "It's about Jesus." "Who's Jesus?" she asked. I asked her if she knew about God and she said "No." My heart broke. I told her about Jesus, starting from Adam and Eve, and asked her if she wanted Jesus to come into her heart. She said, "Yes." It was a precious time.

Some TV people there wanted to do a story about us. After we finished taping, the same little girl came and tugged at my leg and said, "My friends want you to put Jesus into their hearts, too." She had become an evangelist immediately. While we were taping for TV she had gathered her friends to tell them about Jesus.

There must have been nine to 12 children, approximately seven to 12 years old, who had never heard the salvation message of Jesus. So again, it was back to the basics, and they said the sinner's prayer. It was so real to them. You could question them and they knew the answers about salvation. Just as we finished, a little Spanish pastor walked up and we turned the children over to him to continue ministering to them in the future.

The Lord then opened my eyes as I looked up. Diagonally across the street was a denominational church. When we asked them to help with lodging or if they wanted us to speak regarding taking the ministry out of the four walls of the church, encouraging the body of Christ to be bold for Jesus, to be soul winners, they were too busy. I cried—too busy to win the kids on the streets in their neighborhoods for Jesus. What a perfect place for a Saturday street school. The Lord also showed me that besides this church, there were three churches within eye view.

Friends, let's not get so programmed or so busy getting fat in the Word that we forget to win the souls around us. In this day it is rare that we will see people just pop into the church, especially the sinner. We must go where they are and lead them to Jesus and then bring them into the church to help them grow in the things of the Lord. Be a soul winner! The Bible says, *"He that winneth souls is wise"* (Proverbs 12:30).

As we walked from Providence to Pawtucket a man came out of a bar saying, "Jesus never had a wheel on His cross." Russell said, "That's right, but it made you think about Him." We spent a lot of time with him. He said when he was praying the sinner's prayer he felt so light like he thought he was going to fall down. He knew it was real.

We walked by a bus stop and the Lord prompted me to talk to this one girl standing there. As I ministered to her, her eyes filled with tears. She said, "You don't understand, I can't accept Jesus, I've got to sell these drugs." "No you don't," I said, "Jesus can clean you up and change your life, but you have to give Him a chance by receiving Him as your Lord and Savior." She again said, "No, I can't do it now." The bus came but she didn't get on as she wanted to hear more. Three times I asked her to accept Jesus, three times she said, "No, I can't."

Then the Spirit of God came upon me and I prophesied to her that she was going to be in a hard place that could even cost her life and her only way out was to say, "Jesus, help me!" I felt the anointing so strongly. Just then a lady, from one of the churches where we had ministered, stopped and she said she lived in that area and would love to work with this girl. God sets up divine appointments. He gave that girl every chance to accept him, by first sending the cross by her way, then by sending a lady who loved the Lord and wanted to help her.

Walking on, we saw a bunch of kids playing behind this fence. The police sirens went off and they all took off up into the hill behind the area where they were playing. It was full of rocks and thick trees. You couldn't see them. It was like Robin Hood and his merry men. Russell then went into the area where they were playing and yelled out to them to come down, He wanted to talk to them. They wouldn't come so I began to walk up to them. They sent one boy out. I talked to him about Jesus; he didn't even know who Jesus was. I gave him some children tracts and off he ran up to the others with the tracts. How our hearts broke for these young children who knew nothing of God.

We walked on down the street and got to witness to a lot of people who worked at the phone company. They were sitting outside, on their break. They were so receptive to the Gospel. There was a lesbian who looked like a man. She had been in and out of jail. She said that Jesus was her main squeeze. Russell preached hard to her and she broke down crying and truly gave her life to Jesus.

When I see areas where the occult is so strong and New Age is so prevalent, I can only see people who are searching for truth, for something to hold onto that's real! For years so many of the churches have been so dead and without the power of God working in them. They've only become something religious.

I hate religion—that's just of man. Many people have been turned off to Jesus because of just that. They haven't seen any real personal relationships with God. Christianity is about the Father, Son and Holy Spirit! When you see a church operating in the knowledge of the Word, prayer and power, you will see it in the fruit they bear. You will see growth in the church and you will see the Word operating in and through individual lives.

All throughout the New England states we were stopped by occultist people. Many kids who are dabblers into Satanism, and who don't know what they're really getting into, would stop and talk to us. One day this car of several Satanists went past and yelled out, "Satan rules." We just smiled and waved and immediately prayed that the Holy Spirit would reveal the truth of God to them and prayed for their salvation.

When people mocked or showed their hand in any way, we always interceded for their salvation. There was one car that went back and forth past us perhaps six or seven times; the people inside yelled out at us. We yelled back, "Jesus loves you." Then the last time they were getting ready to pass us again. This time I turned my back to them and pointed to what my jacket said, "Jesus loves you." Well that was the last time they passed us. The demons that rule them did not want them to get that message.

We were stopped daily by Jehovah Witnesses. The first few times they stopped we had little knowledge of how to minister to them effectively because we did not have a clear knowledge of their beliefs. So one night we rented *Witness at Your Door* by Jeremiah films. We took precise notes on what they believed. The next day, we were stopped by two young people. The girl was a Jehovah Witness and her boyfriend was studying to be one. We were ready for them; the Holy Spirit gave us all the right words.

With the information we had the night before and what the Bible had to say, we were able to lead that young man to Jesus. All the time the girl was saying, "Don't listen to them, that's all propaganda." We told him to check it out for himself. Then, while we were praying with him, she was talking and trying to pull him away. He told her to leave him alone. He knew what we were saying was truth and he accepted Jesus. Praise the Lord!

Different times as we would be stopped by Jehovah Witnesses or Mormons we were able to find the weaker one or, the one in training, and lead them to Jesus or at least plant seeds on them. It's very important that if you are witnessing to an occult person to know what and why they believe what they do, to minister more effectively to them. If you have no knowledge of their beliefs, do not let them talk to you about it. Simply start off by saying, "Let's pray!" and you do the praying.

People in the occult, first of all, are not allowed to pray with you. Second, they are afraid of your prayers. Most likely they will leave you. If they do not, pray the blood of Jesus to cover you and the Holy Spirit to come into their conversation. Next, never argue their beliefs, because they are so well taught, they can get your believing mixed up if you are not a strong person in the Word and prayer. When ministering to the occult you must be prayed up and strong in the Word! You're not dealing with people as much as you are with the demons that control them.

Strength from Heaven

Rhode Island and Massachusetts are heavy into Satanism and New Age. You can feel the oppression when walking. It was on one of these days, I just didn't feel well. The heat was a scorching hot 100 degrees and the humidity was almost unbearable. Everything in me screamed out to call it quits for today, but the Holy Spirit was pressing us on.

Soon, a Roman Catholic man stopped us. He told us he was 75 years old and that he had been an actor all of his life. He said he wasted most of his life chasing after riches, but now God had saved him and he was working for the Lord. He went on to tell how he was jailed 166 times for helping with "rescues" of the unborn. All of a sudden, he lifted both hands up and began to worship God. He began singing, "Jesus, Jesus, Jesus, There's Just Something about That Name." In the middle of this dark occult area we joined in and we stood there, three people on the side of a busy four lane road, just singing praises to Jesus with our hands lifted up. It was awesome. I know God sent him our way. I felt better and had renewed strength to go on.

As we went down the road, after that, a man spat at us. Many did satanic signs, said, "Satan rules," and mocked us. A few others stopped to have us pray with them. Then a young man came to the cross. He had received Jesus some weeks back. He had a real hunger for Jesus and the Word. In the past few days he had been ready to quit. He had gotten under such oppression he just wanted to give up on life. For several days he couldn't even get out of his house.

In one last ditch effort he prayed, "Father please move on my behalf." All of a sudden he had the urge to get into his car and drive and there was the cross. The Holy Spirit led him to the cross. We were able to pray with him and encourage him with the Word. He left waving and smiling. Thank You, Jesus, for caring so much about what concerns us.

Norwich

A road worker stopped us and said we couldn't walk on US Highway 1. This was the road we had been walking on for weeks. We told him we could; about five minutes later, the police came and said, "You've got to get off of here now." Russell said, "Get off and go where? This is a secondary highway and we can legally walk here and you know it." He kept insisting that we had to get off. Russell said, "Bring the police chief down here." I pulled out the news coverage about the walk. Soon he changed his tune and said he was giving us a police escort. It was great, the devil tried to get us off the road. Now we had a police car with its blue lights flashing following us drawing all kinds of attention to the cross. Then, as we walked into the next town, another police car came out and gave us an escort until we crossed over I-95. Thousands of people saw the cross that day!

Circuit Riding Preacher

It was a beautiful day as we walked through North Attenborough, Massachusetts. A number of people came out to the cross and were ministered to. At one point, I looked up a hill and there sat a beautiful United Methodist Church. I thought to myself, *I would sure like to minister in that church.*

Later that day when Ruthie picked us up, she told us we were going to be ministering at that very church, and that we would just love the pastor and his wife. Back in 1966 Pastor John Camp was one of 12 preachers who carried the Good News Gospel by riding a white horse, wearing a huge black hat, and a long black coat with a white collar, 350 miles from Patten, Maine, to Portland, Maine, to Baltimore, Maryland. He said it was just a fabulous way to witness his love for Jesus. He had great news coverage. Many people came out to him. He was shot at numerous times but was never hurt. I believe that's why he had such a love for our ministry as we had experienced much the same things. What a blessing it was to spend time with him and his church. They had a cookout for us and we had a great time together.

Boston

We walked into Boston, it was beautiful! They have crazy drivers; it was a hard walk; we almost got hit several times. Ruthie called more than

20 churches and asked for a place to stay. She was told there were places like Teen Challenge, Salvation Army, or some homeless places where we could stay. They never took the time to see what we were all about. No room in the inn! I have found out that every time the churches turned us down, the world gladly opened its doors to us.

It was 9:30 at night, still no place to stay. We prayed and drove down the road. I said, "Drive in here." It was a beautiful Holiday Inn. I prayed for favor, went in and spoke to the manager. He gave us the rooms and rolled out the red carpet for us. Anything we wanted was ours. Praise the Lord!

The next day, we had stopped by a phone booth. A man staggered out of his car and looked like he was going to faint. Russell went over and prayed for him and immediately he was healed and the pain that he had was gone. He said he had never felt anything like that before, speaking of being touched by the power of God. Praise God for His wonderful works!

God's Provisions

One wonderful widow lady had us come for lunch. Before we left she loaded us up with a blow up mattress and some blankets along with a couple of pillows. That night we had to sleep on a cold floor. Praise God, He always makes provisions.

We had stopped at a McDonald's and my glasses dropped out of my purse into the parking lot. We drove down the road to start walking the cross when all of a sudden I missed my glasses. So back we went to McDonald's. There they lay in the parking lot with the frames smashed but the lens were okay, not even a scratch. Praise the Lord! We picked them up and prayed that God would have them fixed for me. We drove past a Lens Crafter and took them in and asked what could be done with them. They said they were quite a mess but they would work on them. We prayed, "Father, give them the wisdom and ability to fix them." In time, they handed me my glasses perfectly repaired at no cost. I'm still wearing them now as I write.

One night after ministering, a young lady said the Lord told her to wash my feet. It was such a humbling experience, I cried as she did. She then rubbed them with oil, showing me Jesus' love. I shall never forget that special moment.

Who's Kidding Whom Here?

We crossed the bridge going over to Portsmouth, New Hampshire. It was simply breathtaking, with all the sailboats and yachts. We were asked to stop and minister to the staff at Operation Blessing. It was a very special time for us. As we were leaving we met a young man and his wife who were on fire for Jesus. He proceeded to tell us his story of how he had been arrested many times for passing out tracts. The law says you must have a permit to pass out religious tracts hand to hand. It says nothing about putting tracts on windshields of cars. So he just changed his method of passing out tracts by placing them on every vehicle he would find, including sheriff and police cars. He again was arrested but they couldn't hold him.

Russell and I had personally passed out 3,000 tracts on this walk. It was only the hand of God that has protected us. This young man's statement said, "It's almost like we are in Russia. Our freedom of religion is being stripped from us daily and so few are doing anything about it. Enough is enough! It's time we take our rightful stand. They can pass out condoms to our children in schools but we can't pass out tracts? Who's kidding whom here?" Christian friend, it's time you take your stand for Jesus!

Ogunquit, Maine

It was a hot Saturday and we had a very tiring day walking. We had walked through Kideric where there was a discount mall and a lot of people to see the cross.

Ogunquit was the next resort town and with the busy tourist weekend it seemed almost impossible for Ruthie to locate any lodging for us. When they came to pick us up and told us there was no room, I simply reminded them that God had never failed us yet and that He wasn't going to start now. We prayed and asked for favor. As the four of us got into the van we just began praising God for the victory.

I told Russell that God would show us at which motel to stop. I pointed one out to him and he said, "No, I think we are to keep on driving." Then I spotted a motel and said, "Drive in here." The place was called Milestone Motor Inn. They immediately gave us lodging and opened the door for us to minister in their church the next morning. This is the only Christian Inn in this resort area. It was a wonderful place to stay. They were so kind to us and treated us like kings. It was a great place to rest! God always gives us His best.

The Cocaine House

One night, after ministering, we were asked to spend the night with Jim and LaVone Lessard of York, Maine. We had been told about their lovely home, and were really taken back when we saw it.

This home was a $700,000 house whose prior owner had been sentenced to 55 years for dealing in drugs. It had been put up for auction and was bought by a group of seven people. However, no one ever really lived there for any length of time because of the evil presence the people would feel there. As a result, it sat empty for 10 years.

LaVone heard of this house and went through the records to find the owners. She was told by the owners they weren't interested in selling or even renting it out. As a matter of fact, they turned down $7,000 a month rent that very day. LaVone and Jim saw the house as the perfect place to fulfill the vision they had: a place where ministers and evangelists could come to rest. The house had four stories, 9,000 square feet, two swimming pools, Jacuzzi, decks and a lookout tower that was covered with glass, a perfect place to go to pray. You could see miles from the tower overlooking the coastal area. It was wonderful! They began praying for that house and two days after viewing it with the owners, they got a call back saying they could rent it for $600 in the summer and $500 in the winter. Along with this deal, they would have to care for the house and allow the owners to stay in it, along with them, for 14 days out of the year. This worked out as a tax break for the owners. God is awesome!

LaVone said when you are a faithful tither He will give back to you. You must get past the part of how big the mountain looks and learn to trust Him for even a $700,000 house. LaVone also stated that all the furniture had been given to them. I thank God for this time, it was such a blessing to see faith in action in an ordinary girl's life who chose to believe that the Father was able to give to her, her heart's desire.

Portland, Maine

After months of walking we had reached our goal. There was such an awesome feeling that would come over us as we walked the last mile. I can't describe it. There was no fanfare or bands to welcome us. Yet it was as though the windows of heaven were open saying, "Look! They finished their course!"

On this trip we were on the road five plus months, walking 1,000 plus miles and never missed a meal, always had gas money and a place to stay. Surely we serve a mighty God!

Maine was so beautiful, the trees brilliant with color. It was breathtaking! I thought of my mother many times while walking there. It's always been her heart's desire to visit the New England states in the fall. Perhaps, one day I can bring her here.

We were asked to go back to Camp Shilo to minister at "Escape 92 Music Festival." This was a festival that drew many people from all throughout the New England states. We were blessed to be the main speakers on Sunday morning. They gave us an offering and it was just enough money to fly Randy home to Oregon and to put Ruthie on a bus back to Florida. There were only a few dollars left for gas to get us as far as Pennsylvania. Praising God, for He knew our situation, we headed back to North Brunswick to stay with Alicia and Joe. That night they had their home Bible study group come over. This group was really on fire for Jesus. They boldly witnessed Jesus everywhere they went. What a blessing to see God use and grow the seed you planted.

The next day when we were ready to leave, Alicia said, "Here's my Visa, take and use it to get gas and food to get you home." We never spoke or even hinted of our need to her. God never, ever fails when you walk in obedience to Him and His Word.

Pastors: Don't Quit!

On this trip, more than any other, we ran into so many pastors who wanted to quit. Area after area it seemed we were placed into the homes of hurting pastors. As we would sit and talk, many would break down and cry and say, "It's just too hard." Russell would say, "Quit and go where?" One of the big problems was the apathy of some of the people in the New England states. It was very evident with all the Satanism, witchcraft and New Age movement that many people had given up and quit fighting the warfare battle. We noticed the churches were either on fire for God or struggling.

In many areas, instead of the pastors getting together in love, encouraging one another, praying and playing together, they were isolated from each other. If the devil can keep you off by yourself it's easy for discouragement and loneliness to set in. This goes for any person the devil can isolate. He, then, begins to talk his lies to you.

Remember, we wrestle not against flesh and blood, but against principalities and anything that exalts itself against the name of the Lord our God (Ephesians 6:12). Also, remember that our weapons are not carnal but they are mighty through God to the pulling down of strong holds (2 Corinthians 10:4).

Love your pastor, cover him in prayer daily.

The New England states desperately need our prayers and they need committed people who are called to go there to minister the Gospel.

Arthur Blessitt Joins Us

The Word tells us, "Delight thyself also in the Lord; and He shall give thee the desires of thine heart" (Psalms 37:4).

For years I have desired to walk the cross with Arthur and Denise Blessitt. Arthur is the man who walked the cross around the world through 269 nations and 32,200 miles around the world. He's slept in beds of kings and ministered to national leaders, yet walks humbly on the roads of the world, carrying the simple message of the Gospel of Jesus. His love for Jesus pours out of his whole body. I've never met a man who loved Jesus more than Arthur and, when you're in his presence it's like being with Jesus, as he's taken on His ways.

With a heart of compassion, he and Denise walk through foreign countries on those long hot and dusty roads. With sweat dripping from their faces and bodies that are hot and tired, they keep on walking. For, as far as the eye can see, there are lines of people standing along the edges of the roads waiting to see the cross and hear the message of Jesus.

We love them so much because they're not into big names, although he is one. Nor are they into the material things of life. They are into

Jesus. They have been on a pilgrimage to walk the cross through every nation and country of the world.

We walked with them in the Largo and Clearwater area. Not only were many lives touched that weekend, but I will never be the same. We were asked to go home with them in Naples, Florida. As I lay on the bed that night I cried and thanked God for blessing us with friends like Arthur and Denise and giving us this precious time together.

Arthur and Denise walk in many non-Christian countries and places where you cannot speak the name of Jesus. Pray for their protection, favor and support. They have given up all to follow Jesus. These trips are costly but who can put a price on a soul? You can contact them on Facebook.

Walking the Cross in SW Florida

Russell, Darlene Neptune (a gospel singer), and I walked through Ft. Myers, Naples and Marco Island. We passed out tracts and prayed for many people along the way.

We stopped by the courthouse at Ft. Myers where Russell ministered to three young men. We stood in a circle and prayed the sinner's prayer with them while people walked by, gazing at us. When we were finished, one of the young men said, "That was a cool thing, man, I felt something."

A courthouse is a great place to pass out tracts with lots of people going in and out, and they usually are in need. The bus stop is another great place to pass out tracts. You have a captive audience to minister Jesus. We prayed with a man who we had ministered to earlier at a bus stop and he said, "That was real—I've never felt that before."

You see, people are hungry for something real in their lives. When you witness Jesus, do as the high priests did, cleanse yourselves and pray that the Holy Spirit will move through you to touch someone. Then be real with people, love them where they are with the compassion of Jesus, and you will see great victories (souls being won for the kingdom)! Praise the Lord!

Angel Award Winners

God does all things well! Our original tape, "The Mardi Gras Connection," was a two-hour TV documentary special. We decided to edit it down to a one hour tape and enter it for the Angel Awards.

To edit, we needed editing equipment. We prayed, God heard and Dove Broadcasting invited us to use their equipment. Then there was the $125.00 entry fee to submit the tape. The money was there the day the tape was to be mailed. Praise the Lord!

Next, we needed finances to go to Los Angeles to accept the award if we won. Just a week and a half before we were to leave, some dear friends gave us money to help us. We never asked them; we asked God. Well, this money was needed to pay for the printing of the new picture, "His Glorious Appearing," already promised to the TV-55 Telethon.

Then late the Friday night before the award banquet ceremony, we got the fax saying, "CONGRATULATIONS! YOU ARE AN ANGEL AWARD FINALIST"! We were so excited. We wanted to be there so very much! But we still needed money to go. We decided to sell whatever we could from our storage shed. So, Saturday, we had a roadside yard sale. Still not enough money! We prayed, "Lord, what do we do now?" He prompted our spirits to go, and to trust Him.

So off we headed with about $360. We drove night and day, and just three hours from Los Angeles, our van started making an awful noise. It was night and we were still in the desert. Stopping at a gas station, we were told our air conditioning compressor froze up and if we continued to drive we would cause extensive damage. The report was to get it fixed and don't drive.

We prayed and spent the night in a McDonald's parking lot. The next day we got several estimates, all of which ran about $800, plus. All we had was $42. We did the only thing we knew to do and that was to pray, thank God and ask that the angels would hold it together. As we drove slowly, the sound became worse. We kept thanking God for getting us to California. Well, we made it to Russell's sister's house about 45 miles out of Los Angeles. Her husband, Brian, just happened to be an engineer. He and a friend knew just what to do to fix our van. So off we went. Isn't it wonderful to see God's faithfulness?

When difficult times come, always look for the bright side. While the men were fixing the van, I was able to minister to Brian's friend's wife, and before I left I was able to pray with her about the difficult things happening in her life. PRAISE THE LORD, AGAIN!

What a great time we had at the Angel Awards Banquet. While we were eating, someone handed us a check for $200, and before we left the dinner another check for $40 was presented to us. That's just how it went!

Starting for Home

We left the next day and stayed with a friend in Phoenix, Arizona, and when we were leaving they handed us $60. God is so good! Isn't He? Driving all day, about 4:00 p.m. our radiator hose began to leak and we overheated. We were sitting on top of a mountain. Looking down, we noticed a gas station at the bottom. We prayed and then we coasted down to the door of the gas station garage. The mechanic was ready to leave, but God gave us favor with him and he stayed. It's a good thing we stopped, because our alternator had dropped and by night the belt would have slipped off, leaving us stranded in the desert. Isn't God good? He even gave us the money before we needed it for the repairs and also, we were able to witness Jesus to the mechanic.

You may ask why we are constantly talking about money. Well, it's simply to show you God's faithfulness in our lives. And He is not a respecter of persons. The Bible tells us; so what He does for us, He will do for you. Trust Him! Know Him! Let Jesus be your everything for every situation! Praise Him in the difficult times. Speak the Word over every situation. Don't speak what Satan would have you speak, it's just as easy to speak God's Word. And faith comes by hearing the Word of God.

Looking Back

Looking back over the years of walking, we have learned who our Heavenly Father is. Because of His daily faithfulness to us and His guiding hand in our lives, we will never be the same. Truly, unless you step out in faith and are placed in a position where there are no credit cards or checking accounts and God is you only answer, you will never get to experience this wonderful walk we've had. It is daily trusting Him for your every need!

Ask the Father what it is that He would have you to do. If the vision He gives you is so big that only He can fulfill it, step out in faith and do it. You say, "How do I know that it is God telling me to do this?" Walking the cross seemed to the natural man to be foolish, but that was what He wanted me to do. Don't be led by what your friends or family may say. If you have truly spent time with the Father and you think the vision is of Him, step out in faith and do it. I promise you that, if it's not what

He wants you to do, He will lead you in a different direction. Don't look at the mountain, but rather look how you can go through the mountain with His help.

We will never forget all the many faces, the feel of the wind blowing on our faces, the sounds that, daily, surrounded us, the smells and the white line on the road that we followed for the thousands of miles we walked. The broken people and changed lives will forever be in grafted in our minds.

"Thank You, Lord, for giving us the opportunity to walk the cross and for teaching us who You are. Thank You for Your faithfulness over the years. You've never failed us, not even one time. What an honor it was to have walked this cross for You, proclaiming Your goodness and saving power to the nation. Thank You."

So, You Want to Preach?

Over the years I've had people to tell me, "God has shown me I'm going to be a great evangelist and preach before thousands of people." I say, "Great, what are you doing now to prepare?" "I'm just waiting on the Lord," they say. I answer, "Well, how about going down to the local bus stop or any place where there are people and pass out tracts and tell them how much Jesus loves them and that he has a plan for their lives?" "Oh I couldn't do that because I just don't have the time," some say.

I've heard people say, "I want to be a missionary in Russia." "Great, have you witnessed to your neighbor?" I ask. "Not really, I don't know them well enough to share Jesus. I don't want to offend them after all. I have to live beside them." Others say, "I believe I'm called to be a pastor." "Wonderful!" I say, "Have you cleaned the toilets at your church lately?" "No way!" they say. "Well, perhaps, you should teach Sunday school or help with the children's church or youth ministry?" "I'm not ready," some answer.

Excuses are like arm pits, everyone has two of them and they both stink!

You will never be an evangelist if you can't pass out tracts. You will never be a missionary if you're afraid to witness for Jesus in your own neighborhood. You will never be a pastor without learning how to be a servant. If you feel you have the call of God upon your life to minister in some way and you haven't reached out to others, repent and get on with what God has told you to do. Head in that direction, starting where you are right now and doing what you can to your very best ability, then God will promote you. Be faithful and obedient in the small things so God can give you a bigger job.

You may be reading this and saying, "That lets me off the hook, I'm not called to minister." WRONG! Listen to this: *"Go ye into all the world and preach the gospel to every creature"* (Mark 16:15). Go ye—that's you. Your world is where you are. If you cannot go around the world give money to help others go. This is a command.

Are signs following you? When was the last time you led someone to Jesus? You may say, "Well, I really haven't led anyone to Jesus per se, but I've prayed and given money so others can go and preach." That's all well and good, but you are missing out on the neatest experience you can have and that is leading someone to Jesus. There is no greater joy than that!

Pray this prayer (portions of this prayer are taken from *PRAYERS THAT AVAIL MUCH*):

Dear Father, forgive me for not sharing the Good News Gospel with others when I have had the chance. In the name of Jesus, I am of good courage, I pray that you grant to me that, with all boldness, I speak forth Your Word. I pray that freedom of utterance be given to me that I may open my mouth to proclaim boldly the mystery of the Good News of the Gospel and that I may declare it boldly as I ought to do.

Now begin to take steps to be a witness for Jesus. Pray daily for divine appointments. Declare daily, "I boldly, and in love, speak forth Your Word." Be sensitive to the Holy Spirit moving on you to speak to someone. Now, if you're a real novice, begin by passing out Good News tracts. Always carry tracts with you, pray over them that the convicting power of God will touch the hearts of the people finding the tracts and that they would read them and be saved.

Here are a few examples of how you can place the tracts: when you use a public restroom, leave one in each toilet area or by the sink. Always stuff one up into the condom machine, leaving a small corner visible, so someone will see it and pull it out. If you are really creative, unroll the toilet paper a short way and stick in a tract and roll it back up. Can't you just see the face of the person when that tract comes flying out at them? Go to the newsstand, buy a paper and stick a tract in all the others there. Go to a convenience store, don't read or look at the bad books, just slide a tract into them. I can see the look and feel the chills of a man who proclaims to be a Christian picking up one of those books with a tract in it. It should bring quick repentance. You can go to your local post office and lay them on the counters. I met a lady who writes letters giving the salvation message in it then folds the letter and leaves it lying at the post office. People will always pick it up and read it. There are so many ways to witness for Jesus. Pray and ask Him to give you creative ideas.

You may be sitting there reading this and saying, "I'm just too busy. I don't have time." This is what the Word says:

Then said Jesus unto his disciples, If any man will come after me, let him deny himself, and take up his cross, and follow me.

For whosoever will save his life shall lose it: and whosoever will lose his life for my sake shall find it.

For what is a man profited, if he shall gain the whole world, and lose his own soul? or what shall a man give in exchange for his soul?

For the Son of man shall come in the glory of his Father with his angels; and then he shall reward every man according to his works (Matthew 16:24–27).

If your emphasis is on wealth and riches and you have no time for the Father, I pray the conviction of the Holy Spirit to come upon you. There's coming a day very soon when the heavens will split open and Jesus will be returning for his bride. 1 Thessalonians 4:16–17 states:

> For the Lord Himself shall descend from heaven with a shout, with the voice of the archangel, and with the trump of God: and the dead in Christ shall rise first.
>
> Then we which are alive and remain shall be caught up together with them in the clouds to meet the Lord in the air: and so shall we ever be with the Lord.

Will you be ready? Will you just enter heaven with your salvation? What will you take with you? Will you stand before the Lord empty handed?

Please note there is nothing wrong with great riches and things. The point is, do you own the things or do they own you? It takes a lot of money to spread the Gospel. My concern is for you, my friend.

I knew a lady of great wealth. She was a dear friend and at one time I was in her will. She was so upset with me for giving up everything to walk the cross that she took me out of her will. She died and her money stayed here. She couldn't take any of it with her. Just think how that could have been used to spread the Gospel!

If your riches own you as they once owned me, it's sin, because you'll be too busy for God! However, I know some very wealthy people who love God with their whole heart and, as a result, God has greatly prospered them. I guess what I'm trying to say is "seek ye first." God wants to prosper you in all your ways. He wants to make you a blessing so that you can be a blessing. Just fall in love with Jesus! When you do, everything else is secondary. What's in your heart will come out of your mouth. The best witness is your own testimony and what God is doing through you.

We have met complete strangers and shared the good things God has done in our lives and they received Jesus. Most people who don't know Jesus are searching for an answer and when you come along with a smile on your face and simply share the goodness of Jesus, it's what they need to hear. Don't preach at them, you will turn them off. Also, don't go out witnessing looking dirty or like a rag bag. Who wants that kind of Jesus? Remember, the Holy Spirit is neat and clean. Be a good example of the One living inside of you! Always be ready to witness for Jesus wherever you are; in the gas station, in the store, in a checkout line, getting the car oil changed, in the video store or in an elevator. Russell and I have personally led people to Jesus in all of these places; just be sensitive to the tugging of the Holy Spirit. Swallow that pride, because it's pride that will keep you from sharing the goodness of Jesus. Be bold and always remember; if you're witnessing to someone who's working, to keep it very short. It's not right to steal that employer's time.

If someone stops and asks you for directions, give it to them along with directions on how to get to heaven. You are the only witness many people will ever see. Ask God for His wisdom to be the best witness for Him that you can be. Someone's eternal life may depend on you being a willing vessel. If you saw a house burning and there was a small child in the house, you would risk your life to rescue that child. There are people all around you, dying and going to hell. What are you doing to rescue them? Ask God to give you a burden for souls.

The Bible says that he who wins souls is wise. Be a wise man, be a soul winner. In writing this book, it has not been to glorify us or what we've done, but to show the goodness and faithfulness of God. My heart's desire is that you will be encouraged, first, to love the Lord your God with all your heart and, second, to get a burden for souls. He's looking for vessels whom are willing to be used for his service. Seek the Lord for what He would have you to do, and head in that direction. Stay single minded to that goal and remember always be a witness for Jesus.

Walking in Constant Victory

In writing this book, I have tried to show you the goodness and mercy of God through our trials and victories. I have opened ourselves up to you so you could see our shortcomings as well as our triumphs. Did you know God wants you always to walk in constant victory? This will come when you know who you are in Christ Jesus.

Meet Who You Are in Christ Jesus

1. YOU ARE RIGHTEOUS.

You have right standing with God because of what Jesus did. Second Corinthians 5:21 says, *"For He (God) hath made Him (Jesus) to be sin for us, who knew no sin; that we might be made the righteousness of God in Him."* This clearly shows Jesus paid the price for your sins. Righteousness comes through faith in God. The price Jesus paid for our sins is enough. It is not through our performance that we are accepted by God.

Ephesians 2:8–9 says, *"For by grace are ye saved through faith, and that not of yourselves: it is the GIFT of God: Not of works, lest any man should boast.*" I am not talking about religion, but about a personal relationship with Jesus.

There is nothing bad enough that you could have done that can keep you from coming to God. There is nothing good enough that you could do, to be accepted. It's only based on Jesus and your acceptance of Him. *"To the praise of the glory of His grace, through which He hath made us ACCEPTED IN THE BELOVED"* (Ephesians 1:6).

2. YOU ARE DELIVERED.

You have been delivered from the power of darkness and are joint heirs with Jesus according to Colossians 1:12–13: "Giving thanks unto the Father, who hath made us meet (fit) to be partakers of the inheritance of the saints in light; who hath delivered us from the power of darkness, and hath translated us into the kingdom of His dear Son." Everything God has, you have. You are no longer under the dominion of darkness. The devil no longer has power of over you. Sickness, poverty, fear, and depression must go. Get off the devil's mailing list and return those defeats to the sender, the devil.

3. YOU ARE BLESSED.

You are blessed beyond all you could ever think. The promises of God define your inheritance. Read Deuteronomy 28. Galatians 3:29 says, *"And if ye be Christ's, then are ye Abraham's seed, and heirs according to the promise."* Find out about the blessings. Read Matthew 5:3–16. Learn about your inheritance. It is all in the Word, the Bible.

4. YOU ARE WISE.

You can make right decisions because you are plugged in to God. James 1:5 says, "If any of you lack wisdom, let him ask of God, that giveth to all men liberally (generously), and upbraideth not, and it shall be given him." You can also read Colossians 1:28.

5. YOU ARE A WINNER—ALL THE TIME!

Get your mind transformed out of a defeated attitude and into being a winner. You are what you think. Proverbs 23:7 says, *"For as he thinketh in his heart, so is he."*

You must see yourself as a winner. I Corinthians 15:57 says, *"But thanks be to God who giveth us the VICTORY through our Lord Jesus Christ."* You win, because you are in Him and He is in you.

"If God be for us, who can be against us?" (Romans 8:31). Romans 8:35 says, "Who shall separate us from the love of Christ! Shall tribulation, or distress, or persecution, or famine, or nakedness, or peril, or sword?" Verse 37 says, "Nay, in all these things we are more than conquerors through Him that loved us." As you can see in these verses, in all natural and physical things we are more than conquerors through Jesus. "Now thanks be unto God, which always causeth us to triumph in Christ" (2 Corinthians 2:14). "I can do all things through Christ which strengtheneth me" (Philippians 4:19).

Our lives have been enriched in every area through Jesus. Many times our perception of things is warped. We tend to allow our environment and circumstances to affect how we think and the way we do things. We must renew our minds to what the Word has to say about our situation. The storms of life may come but you can go through those storms and be standing afterwards. Do not glory in the storms, but in the God Who will get you through the storms. When you know the Word you can have perfect peace through the storms.

It is hard to build a foundation on the Word when you are in the midst of the storm or trial. Our foundation, or beginning, must first be built on Jesus Christ. I Corinthians 3:11 says, *"For other foundation can no man lay than that which is laid, which is Jesus Christ."*

Then you must have a strong spirit full of faith in the Word to pull you through the storm. Proverbs 18:14 says, *"The spirit of a man will sustain his infirmity (weakness or inability to produce results), but a wounded spirit who can bear it?"*

Ephesians 4:22–24 says, *"That ye put off concerning the former conversation (manner of life) the old man, which is corrupt according to the deceitful lusts, and be renewed in the spirit of your mind; and that ye put on the new man, which after God is created in righteousness and true holiness."*

Your mind must be renewed to what the Word says for you to have victory. The Word produces faith (Romans 10:17) and faith will cause you to be an overcomer.

I John 5:4–5 says, *"For whatsoever is born of God overcometh the world; and this is the victory that overcometh the world, even our faith. Who is he that overcometh the world, but he that believeth that Jesus is the Son of God."*

Your faith will not go past your question marks. For example: "Is it God's will for me to be healed?" Faith begins when the will of God is known. You can know God's will when you learn about your inheritance and the promises God has given you in the Word.

A wonderful example of faith is found in Matthew 7:24–27. This is the parable of two builders and two foundations. Both of these builders heard the same Word. The one applied the word of faith and built his house on the rock, the Word of God, and when the storms came, he was at perfect peace and comfort. The second one's house was built on the sand because he never applied the word of faith that he heard, and never put the Word in his heart, so great was his fall.

The house here represents ourselves. The choice is yours, you can either be an overcomer or be overcome. Many people have Bibles everywhere in their homes, but if they never study the Word and put it to work in their lives, they are like the man who built his house on the sand. To be an overcomer and live in constant victory, you need the power of God to work through you. You can have the divine power of God working all the time in your life, just listen to this. Second Peter 1:3–4 says, "According as his divine power HATH GIVEN unto us ALL THINGS that pertain unto LIFE AND GODLINESS, through the knowledge of him that hath called us to glory and virtue; By which are given unto us

EXCEEDING GREAT and PRECIOUS PROMISES, that by THESE YE MIGHT BE PARTAKERS OF THE DIVINE NATURE."

When I was sixteen, I was given a Bible by my parents which, by the way, I still have. On the front inside pages I wrote, *"For I am not ashamed of the gospel of Christ; for it is the power of God to everyone that believeth"* (Romans 1:16). This has been my theme verse all my life. For years I used that as my verse to proclaim the gospel and goodness of Jesus Christ, being a bold witness wherever I went, be it a convenience store, gas station, restaurant, the streets, wherever there were people.

Recently, I have learned of another meaning to this verse from the best teacher of the Word I know, Pastor Tim Gilligan. I was so excited about it that I wanted to share it with you. The Word says, *"I am not ashamed of the Gospel of Jesus Christ"*—Christ means Anointed One and refers to the anointing as seen in Luke 4:18, *"The SPIRIT of the Lord is upon me, because he hath anointed me to preach the gospel to the poor; he hath sent me to heal the brokenhearted, to preach deliverance to the captives, and recovering the sight to the blind, to set at liberty to them that are bruised."*

The Gospel of Jesus Christ is the Good News of the complete plan. Salvation is all things which pertain to life and godliness, as well as forgiveness for our sins and a home eternally in heaven. The Bible says, *"It is the POWER OF GOD UNTO SALVATION TO EVERYONE WHO BELIEVES."*

Secrets of Faith

We plug into the power of God unto salvation (remember all that salvation means) by BELIEVING. There are some people who are all around the power, but they are not plugged in. You MUST get your believing right, by renewing your mind to what the Word says, and get the Word into your heart. There can be two people side by side and hear the same

Word. One only heard it while the other one mixed faith with the Word he heard (Hebrews 4:2).

Faith, or what you are believing, comes out of your mouth. "A good man, out of the good treasure of his heart, bringeth forth that which is good; and an evil man out of the evil treasure of his heart bringeth forth that which is evil: for out of the ABUNDANCE OF THE HEART HIS MOUTH SPEAKETH" (Luke 6:45).

What are you saying: Faith filled words or doubt and unbelief? Record what you are saying and just listen to the words of your mouth and you can locate your faith level. Your confession (what you are saying) locates your faith.

The power of God unto salvation is available to all, but it's not automatic. You must plug in by faith. Mark 11:22 says, "Have faith in God." Verse 23 goes on to say, "For verily I say unto you, That whosoever shall say unto this mountain, be thou removed, and be thou cast into the sea; and shall not doubt in his HEART, but shall BELIEVE that those THINGS which he SAITH shall come to pass, HE SHALL HAVE WHATEVER HE SAITH." Nothing happens until whosoever says.

You release God's power working by putting the Word in your heart and by speaking it. Get off that old religious thinking that says, "You're just one of those name it and claim it people." It is what the Word clearly says for you to do to have victory in your life. It says, "YOU SHALL HAVE WHATSOEVER YOU SAY." So why not line up with what the Word has to say about your situation instead of glorifying the problem?

The book of wisdom, Proverbs, has a lot to say about the power of the tongue. For instance, Proverbs 18:21 says, "Death and life are in the power of the tongue, and they that love it shall eat the fruit thereof." This verse clearly states what comes out of your mouth will bring you life or death.

I suggest that you read James Chapters 1, 2 and 3, especially chapter 3:3–11. If you have never been taught about the power of the tongue, these chapters and verses will open your eyes. I also recommend that you read Charles Capp's book, THE TONGUE—A CREATIVE FORCE. It will change how you talk.

If you change your talk, you can change your walk. Remember, the Word says you shall have whatever you say, that can be for good or bad.

Again, it's what you believe in your heart that will come out of your mouth. Second Corinthians 4:13 says, "We, having the same spirit of faith, according as it is written, I BELIEVED, AND THEREFORE HAVE I SPOKEN; we also believe and therefore speak."

To be saved, you had to confess Jesus as it states in Roman 10:9–10, "with the mouth confession is made unto salvation." The best place to hear the Word is out of your own mouth. It is a proven fact, that if you should tell a lie long enough, you, yourself, will believe the lie. How much more does this principle work when you speak what is absolute truth, the Word of God! If you CONFESS THE WORD over and over again, it will take root in your heart and you will believe what you are saying and hearing. Faith cometh by hearing and hearing the Word.

This is not a "works thing," it is simply coming into agreement with what the Word says. For example: if you have financial failures and you continually speak of them, you are coming into agreement with the failure. However, if you begin to speak the prosperity promises, soon your faith level will rise and your situation will change.

You need to shatter those images of poverty and lack that you now see yourself in, and replace them with a vision of you prospering according to what the Word says. Philippians 4:19 says, "But my God SHALL SUPPLY ALL YOUR NEED according to his riches in glory by Christ Jesus." This is only one of many verses that you need to speak out of your mouth daily.

Joshua 1:8 says, "This book of the law shall not depart out of thy mouth, but thou shall MEDITATE therein DAY and NIGHT, that thou mayest observe to do according to all that is written therein; for THEN THOU SHALT MAKE THY WAY PROSPEROUS, AND THEN THOU SHALT HAVE GOOD SUCCESS."

What are you meditating on day and night? The soaps on TV, movies, nightly TV programs, the news? By the way, for the most part, the newsmen are not walking in the ways of the Lord, but rather in the ways of darkness, and will tell you all the bad news, instead of the good, so why use that for your source of information when you can hear the good news from the Word of God?

The news may tell you for example, that this is going to be the worst year for the flu season. The chances of you catching it will be one in two. I don't receive that bad report because according to the Word you can walk in divine health, "For by His stripes you have already been healed" (1 Peter 2:24). However, if you haven't meditated on the Word, you could receive the seed of that bad report. Do you see what I am trying to tell you?

Don't use the news for your source of information. Use what the Word says. You ask, "Are you saying I shouldn't watch the news?" No, just don't feed or meditate on it. Meditate on the Word. Read about Smith Wigglesworth; he wouldn't let ten minutes go by without meditating on the Word in some way. As a result, his words had such power that he raised the dead on numerous occasions as well as healed the sick. You see, he was so full of the Word that all that came out of his mouth was the Word. No doubt or unbelief.

You can have as much of God and His power working through you as you want. It's strictly up to you. It does not come without paying a price. What are you putting before your eyes or listening to with your ears? Remember, you are like a computer, "Garbage in, garbage out." Put the Word of God in, then speak the Word of God out, and it will work for you.

Also, spending much time in communication with the Father plays a big part here. Who are you in love with? It will show in and through your life, by what comes out of your mouth and by whom and what you are spending your time with. This is work, my friends, it doesn't just come to you, it is something you must do for yourself, by getting into the Word and digging out the promises of God and spending that special time with Him daily.

If watching too much TV is a stronghold in your life, try turning it off for twenty one days and go on a TV fast; replace it with time in the Word and fellowship with the Father. It would be good to take the phone off the hook and turn off the computer and your cell phone during the hours you spend in the Word, because you can count on the devil to bring interruptions during this time. He knows you are about to hook into the power of God like you never were before and, therefore, you will be a threat to him and his kingdom. By the way, it takes twenty one days to break a habit or to form a new one.

You may say, "I've tried this confession thing, but it never worked for me." Many people give up just before the victory comes. It is not a trying thing, it is a lifestyle. Keep on keeping on, until victory comes. Now faith must have a corresponding action.

1. FAITH—(believing) is the plug to the power.
2. CONFESSION—We release the power of faith through our confession.
3. ACTION—Faith has action. Faith without works is dead (James 2:17).

Reasoning something out always messes up your faith. Just keep it in your heart. If the Word says it, I believe it. This is not a head thing, it is a heart thing.

Now that we have the Word of faith in our heart, we then confess it with our mouth, and then we take action on it. Good examples are found all throughout the four Gospels. Example: the lady with the issue of blood. She had faith and said that if she could just touch the hem of Jesus' garment, then she knew that she would be healed. She pushed her way through the crowd of people and reached out and touched Jesus and she was healed. That took action (Mark 5:25–34).

How about the four men who took off the roof of a house where Jesus was teaching to lower the sick man? He was healed. That, too, took action (Mark 2:1–12). It still works the same today.

Remember, in the earlier chapters, when I spoke about how we received our last van? We prayed for one, we went out and found what we wanted (action). We told them that God would supply the money as His Word says that He meets all our needs. Several days later when we went back they said they had sold it, and what was our reply? "You can sell it as much as you want, but this is still our van!" We had the word of faith that the Father told Russell this was our van. Now, at this point, we could have changed our confession and lost the van, however, we held on with the confession of our faith and never one time released it with our words. A week later God did supply the money and we drove off with the van. That is faith in action.

Ephesians 3:20 says, "Now unto Him who is able to do EXCEED-INGLY ABUNDANTLY above ALL that we ask or think, ACCORD-ING TO THE POWER THAT WORKETH IN US."

Third John 1:2 says it like this, "Beloved (that's you) I wish above all things that you may prosper and be in health (that's the natural) even as your soul prospereth (having the Word in your heart)."

Those verses make it quite clear that it is all up to you. How much of God do you want operating in your life? You can sit idly by and see others prosper in the things of God or you can get plugged in through faith and have constant victory in your life. Get plugged in! Your life will be changed and you will be a world changer forever!

SPECIAL NOTE: Much of what I have shared with you in this chapter came from the teaching messages of Tim Gilligan, pastor of Meadowbrook Church in Ocala, Florida. We have met and heard many of the great teachers of the Word, but truly, I can say none have taught it so simply or made it come so alive for application in today's life as Pastor Tim has. Our lives have totally changed and grown because of this great pastor!

Have You Heard the Good News?

When asked the question, "Where will you spend all eternity?" most people say they hope or think they'll spend it in Heaven. They're not positive where they will go.

First John 5:12–13 says, "He who has the Son has life, and he who does not have the Son of God does not have life. I write these things to you who believe in the name of the Son of God so that you may know that you have eternal life."

It is a common misconception that, by being baptized or by doing good works, you will be guaranteed a place in Heaven. Jesus said in John 3:3, "Verily, verily, I say unto thee, except a man be born again he cannot see the kingdom of God."

It is not what we have done but what God has done for us that will secure our salvation. Ephesians 2:8 says, "For by grace are ye saved through faith, and that not of yourselves; it is the gift of God."

Eternal Life, or salvation is a free gift from God; you cannot earn it.

It takes more than just believing there is a God to secure salvation. The Bible says that even the demons in hell believe there is a God and yet they will not be saved.

The answer is in Romans 10:9–10; "That if thou shalt confess with thy mouth the Lord Jesus and shalt believe in thine heart that God hath raised Him from the dead, thou shalt be saved. For with the heart man believeth unto righteousness; and with the mouth confession is made unto salvation."

Salvation comes through believing that Jesus is the Son of God and confessing Him as Lord. If you don't know Jesus as your personal Lord and Savior, you can accept Him right now. This is the first step you must take to have constant victory.

He will fill your life with a peace and joy that only He can give. You can have a victorious, prosperous life and a home in Heaven forever. He doesn't care about your past or the sins you've committed. He doesn't care if you've been a prostitute, thief, drug dealer, murderer or a good guy who has never made Jesus your Lord.

Second Corinthians 6:2 says, "Now is the day of salvation."

When you ask Jesus to come into your life, you are instantly born again. The old you is gone, you are a new creature (2 Corinthians 5:17).

All your old past has been washed away. It's like putting dirt on your hands and washing it off, you can never go down the drain and get that dirt and put it back on your hands, as it is forever gone. So it is when we repent of our sins, they are forever gone. When the devil tries to remind you of your past, just remind him of what the Word says about you and remind him of his future.

If you believe Jesus is the Son of God and that He died for your sins and rose again, you can know for sure that you'll go to Heaven. If you pray this prayer and mean it with all your heart, you shall be saved and know you have eternal life.

PRAY THIS OUT LOUD, RIGHT NOW:

God in Heaven; I know I'm a sinner and I need Your help.
I believe in my heart that Jesus Christ is Your Son,

that He died on the cross for my sins
and that You raised Him from the dead.
Jesus, right now I open my heart and invite You to come in.
Make Yourself real to me. Take control of my life.
Keep me from evil and make me the person You want me to be.
Be my Lord and Savior. Amen!!!

Sign_____
Date_____

If you have just made Jesus your Lord, you are now born again and you are going to Heaven. Tell someone about your new walk with Jesus contact me. I would love to hear from you.

Write to:

Dorothy Luscombe Spaulding
Watchmen Broadcasting
P.O. Box 3618
Augusta, GA 30914-3618
(803) 278-3618
E-mail at:club36@wbpi.org
Website: wbpi.org

Note: Watch us daily on Club 36 on Watchmen Broadcasting
10:00 a.m.—12:00 noon—Live Broadcast
8:00 p.m.—10:00 p.m.
Midnight—2:00 a.m.

Watch us on the internet at wbpi.org. Check out our Facebook page—WBPITV49 and again on Facebook Live at the times above. Watch on Roku—Watchmen Broadcasting and Glorystar TV.

Watchmen Broadcasting: Our Walk by Faith Continues

The Journey of Watchmen Broadcasting began in 1995. After eight miracle filled years of walking the cross around America, Russell and I felt the prompting of God to begin a Christian television station in Augusta, Georgia.

After taking a month off from walking the cross to write this book, I felt the Lord say, "Open a station in Augusta, Georgia." For years while walking the cross our dear friend asked us to open a station in Augusta, Georgia. We always said no because it wasn't what God told us to do. Now the Lord was saying to me to open this new station. I spoke to Russell about it. He said, "The next time we go to Greenville we can pass through Augusta and see what the Lord says." As we drove into the city of Augusta, Georgia, I heard the Lord say to me, "This is where I want you." Russell said he felt the same thing.

With our commitment to God made to come to Augusta and less than $100, we began to work out of the Days Inn on Washington Road so as to raise awareness and community involvement in the area. One obstacle had to be overcome, where to house the vision of the future network. Having secured the tower-site, we began driving around to find a suitable location for the studio.

As we were driving up Knox Avenue in North Augusta, again the Lord spoke and said, "This is your building." Our faith was put to the test immediately when the owner quoted the monthly price of $7,000. With another figure in our hearts, we went to return the keys after viewing the building. Immediately we drove back to the building, anointed it with oil and said, "You belong to God and there will be a television station here promoting the gospel 24/7." We then asked the owner if we could hold a one-time event in the building on July 21, 1995. Calls were made and invitations sent, thus the stage was set for Open House. Just three days before the event the owner of the building agreed to the event and the $2,000 per month figure that God had laid on our hearts. After trading and bartering for just a few days, preparations were complete for the big night and the filming of the very first Club 36 on July 21, 1995. With pastors, fellow believers, community leaders, and special guests at a still empty building, the vision for the future worldwide ministry began to be revealed. Opening night was a complete success. However, later that night, the owner of the television license pulled me aside and informed me that participating in the vision of raising up Augusta, Georgia would be too big for them to participate in, as he just got Atlanta. I went to God and said, "Why did he send us here." God said, "He didn't, I did. Build my station." With another test of our commitment to God's mandate, I stood firm and asked if they could raise the station by faith. The owner of the license replied, "Yes."

After concluding the successful opening night, the next obstacle for the very young ministry was to get on the airways. The Transmitter was in place but we needed to get on the air. We met a satellite man, Anthony, and he hooked a satellite directly to the transmitter and TV-36 was on the air. Next the device needed to send the signal from the studios to the tower was yet to be purchased. The STL or Studio Transmitter Link, which was needed, had a hefty price tag of $8,000. I contacted the owners of the license and asked if they could help but found out they could not. Not sure how to resolve the situation, Russell and I prayed for wisdom and came into agreement that the need would be met. About 4:00 that day, I received a call from a gentleman who asked what the station needed. My response was $8,000. The gentleman then replied, "You've got it." From that very moment forward, miracle after miracle began to take place.

We needed lumber and a man called and asked if we could use a truck load of lumber. The answer was yes. Weekly we held prayer meetings from the first week we were in the building calling things that were not as if they were. We were given a production truck Monday through Friday with all the equipment needed to produce our two-hour nightly live program, Club 36. I called all the local networks, speaking to the engineers and asked them for any old equipment they had that we could use. We received all kinds of equipment from record decks and players, switches, sound equipment, lights, microphones, etc. Our dear friend, Claud Bowers of WACX—Channel 55 in Orlando, Florida, brought a truck load of equipment to us; plus he sent us his engineer at no charge to us.

From pastors to local businesses and ministries, materials and labor began to pour in. From lumber to paint, furniture to equipment, support came from everywhere. Sets began to take from, nightly production became the norm, and lives began to be changed.

Month after month, year after year, the station TV-36 saw expansion and growth. In 2000, Russell and I were able to buy the license because friends across the nation gave us the money. We named the new network Watchmen Broadcasting, a name God gave Russell years before.

In 2001, with an FCC requirement, the 36 channel line use was moved from Augusta and given to another city. Almost daily I would call the FCC in Washington, DC to ask what needed to happen. After months of calling, the FCC gave specific instructions and I followed them. As with previous years, God made a way. The station went from

TV-36 to TV-49 moving from 1,000 watts of power to 150,000 watts of power. Increasing the potential viewership, TV-49 not only expanded with its over-the-air coverage but with local cable systems as well, being picked up by three of the four major cable systems in the Central Savannah River Area (CSRA).

Watchmen Broadcasting's desire to reach the world with unique Christian programming began to take place in 2002 with the launch of Roc House Café, locally. Then in 2003, Roc House went national and finally in 2004, international. Following Roc House Café came By the Book, going national that same year and international in 2004. Both Roc House Café and By the Book continue to make their mark to this day having received multiple Angel, Telly, and Davy Awards.

A further test of the resolve of the ministry came in 2006, when the station's transmitter was hit and all but destroyed by lightning. Functioning with only 10 percent power for the next four months, God began to work another miracle for Watchmen Broadcasting to purchase one of the industry's best transmitters. The new transmitter enabled TV-49 to transmit its signal stronger and farther than ever. Then in 2009, the mandate from the FCC came down from Washington, DC. This mandate offered another chance for God's faithfulness to be shown. In January 2009, with not all finances raised, deadlines were moved and God placed it on the hearts of many across the CSRA and America to make sizeable donations so that TV-49 could complete its FCC mandated digital upgrade, and so the story has been with Watchmen Broadcasting, miracles, signs, and wonders. Every time it looked like failure would be the final word, God always stepped in and made a way. Why? With 21 years of ministry, thousands of salvations, thousands of suicide prevention calls, and over a million ministry calls answers that question. Watchmen Broadcasting, 21 years later is still television that changes lives.

In January of 2013, we heard the message according to the Israel year of 5773 that the Camels are Coming and come they did. We were given $604, 000 to buy the building. We were all so excited! I called the owner of the building and told him Jesus sent the money to buy the building at the $600,000, agreed price. He said the price of the building went up to $1,500,000. My answer was that if God wanted us to pay that price He would have sent that amount. We tried to work with him for two months. So, after prayer, I called the owner of the Food Lion next door. His building was on the market for $1,200,000. I offered him $400,000. His answer was, "I have always wanted you to have this building." The Food Lion building was purchased. This 33,000 square foot building had all the copper stolen out of the air conditioner, the electricity was stripped out and the roof needed to be replaced.

Through all these years of hard times and good times, Quit has never been an option. We must press on to complete what God has called us to do. It's all about souls for the Kingdom, changed lives. Then one day when we stand before God we will hear Him say, "Well done, thou good and faithful servant." That is Russell and my desire. God has raised up Tamara and Chris, my daughter and son-in-law, to follow in our footsteps with the same burden for people as we have. I praise Him. Never give up on God. He is faithful! It is still a walk by faith.

Wow! What a major undertaking as we have now stripped the building. All that is left are the bare walls. The roof has been replaced. Now we face the rebuilding from the floor up. With God we can do all things. It will take about $3.5 million more to finish our new building. If you wish to help us with this project, please donate now to:

Watchmen Broadcasting
P.O. Box 3618
Augusta, GA 30914
(803) 278-3618

WATCHMEN BROADCASTING
MEDIA THAT CHANGES LIVES

Watch Club36 daily with host Dorothy Spaulding
10am - 12pm | 8pm - 10 pm | 12am - 2am EST

DOWNLOAD OUR MOBILE APP

1. Open your app store
2. Search "Church App Tithe.ly"
3. Download the blue app
4. Search "Watchmen Broadcasting"
5. Click "Change"

OTHER WAYS TO WATCH WATCHMEN BROADCASTING

Facebook Live - WBPI TV 49
YouTube
Roku - Watchmen Broadcasting
Glorystar.tv

For more information call
803.278.3618

Paintings by Dorothy Luscombe Spaulding

The Bride 16" x 20"

By His Stripes 16" x 20"

His Glorious Appearing
16" x 20"

Your Royal
Wedding Invitation
With DVD "What
To Do If You Miss
the Rapture."
by Perry Stone